Selected as Outstanding by Parent Council®

This book is a wonderful guide for parents who want to speak to their children of all ages with the true authority of compassion, intelligence, and understanding. It tells us what to say, how to say it, when to say it, and why to say it. Deceptively simple, this book is full of good ideas that could change the world. — *Joanna Robinson, parent*

You can still be the parent you always dreamed of being. Gary Screaton Page shows you how to reclaim a common sense approach and learn positive communication . . .straightforward and entertaining.
— *Lisa Wroble, Parenting Today's Teen*

A great deal of common sense approaches to dealing with one's child.
— *The Voice of Pelham*

This book helps parents identify the parenting style that works best for them. It teaches them how to communicate within their chosen styles and according to their personal values. — *The Tribune, Welland ON*

A helpful guide for parents of children of all ages who feel that they don't have positive relationships with their children. — *Youth Today*

Every parent, teacher, and caregiver, no matter how skillful, has something significant to gain from Gary Page's insights and recommendations for better communication with children ... continuing throughout life. Highly recommended reading.
— *Jim Cox, Midwest Book Review*

My daughter was spiraling downward. Not only were her grades and study habits deteriorating, she was withdrawing from all communication. I changed my approach immediately after reading this book. The results have been dramatic. Thank you. — *Lin Smith, parent*

This practical book offers tremendous input for both parents and teachers. I have benefited greatly from reading this book, and so have my three children and many students!
— *Tim Bedley, Mr. Tim's Tips for New Teachers*

Communication with my son has improved significantly thanks to practicing the concepts in this book. I realized a lot of the struggles we've been having are because I've been using a heavily "My Way" parenting style, which is no longer appropriate for his age. I'm starting to use more "Our Way" and "Your Way" decision making when appropriate. I am looking forward to the rest of the book, since I am getting very encouraging results from the first 96 pages!
— *Terry Shafer, parent*

After taking the parental style survey in this book and finding myself in the "My Way" category (thinking I was an "Our Way" parent), I rethought how I talk to my daughter. The subject of laundry is a common problem. Using a skill I learned, my daughter responded by writing a contract herself, stating she would do laundry on Wednesday. We both signed it and shook on the deal. I agreed not to nag her. To my amazement she has done her laundry two weeks in a row, without a word from me. I will be recommending this to others!

— Chris Kucala, parent

As a parent, I would jump in and scold my children every time a problem came up. This created angry arguments and sometimes resentment that lasted for days. Gary Page's book certainly helped change this situation. It offers specific examples and an easy-to-follow communication skills program that parents can customize to fit their own parenting styles. I wish this book had been available years ago.

— Duane Newcomb, parent

Gary Page has captured the communication skills that parents need to create an open dialogue with their children. I've used these skills with my teenagers. They really work!! My fourteen- and seventeen-year-old sons still talk to me, and I know it is because of these fabulous skills.

— Miriam Georg, parent

I looked through dozens of books on parenting for help with my teenage son. This book could not have arrived at a better time. I read the first couple of chapters and applied the skills I learned. Within two days he began to respond and his mood brightened. Within two weeks we were talking the way we did before he became a teenager. The communication skills in this book not only make you a better parent, they make you a better person.   *— Judy Phillips, parent*

What is unique about this book over other parenting guides on the market is that Page doesn't make a judgment about a person's parenting style. Instead, the book is geared to all parenting styles. He presents his 12 communication skills in clear language. If you follow each of his communication skills and work through the examples and exercises, you will communicate more effectively with your children and be the parent (and teacher) you want to be.

— Marjan Glavac, The Busy Educator's Newsletter

Being the Parent
YOU Want to Be:
12 Communication Skills
for Effective Parenting

Being the Parent YOU Want to Be

12 Communication Skills for Effective Parenting

by
Gary Screaton Page, M.Ed.

Performance Learning Systems
Nevada City, California

Performance Learning Systems, Publications Division, Nevada City, CA 95959
© 1999 by Performance Learning Systems, Inc.
All rights reserved. Published 1999
Printed in the United States of America
10 9 8 7 6 5 4 3 2

Unless specifically stated as real in the text, similarity to real names and/or events is purely coincidental.

PLS Bookstore
224 Church Street
Nevada City, CA 95959
www.plsbookstore.com
info@plsbookstore.com
800-506-9996

Library of Congress Cataloging-in-Publication Data

Page, Gary Screaton. 1942-
    Be the parent you want to be: 12 communication skills for
effective parenting / by Gary Screaton Page.
       p. cm.
    Includes bibliographical references and index.
    ISBN 1-892334-07-0 (pbk. : alk. paper)
    1. Parent and child.   2. Communication in the family.
3. Parenting.   4. Interpersonal communication.   I. Title.
HQ755.85.P34   1999   98-45965
649'.1--dc21   CIP

Cover design: Brook Design Group
Interior design: Donna Burke
Illustrations: Helen Strang
Index: Brackney Indexing Service
Author's photograph: Thies Bogner

This book may be ordered from the PLS Bookstore, 224 Church Street, Nevada City, CA 95959. 800-506-9996. Quantity discounts are available for bulk purchases, sales promotions, premiums, fund-raising, and educational needs.

DEDICATION

To the thousands of young people I've had the privilege to teach, and to my children, Jason and Deidre: you taught me most of what I know about children.

To Paul, who was in my first class of grade fives, and who, when the time came, asked me to be his Best Man: you taught me to let children know where I stand, and that it's important to let them make up their own minds as they grow.

To Julie, Debbie, and many others who have confirmed my decision to teach: you forgave my mistakes, for which I'll always be grateful.

God bless you all.

CONTENTS

FOREWORD

Parenting today, while challenging, holds greater hope than ever. We simply know more about how to develop good communication between people in general, and between adults and children in particular.

This helpful, easy-to-read book by Gary Page comes from results he got while holding parenting courses. From years of counseling both parents and children, he realized that many problems in families happen because parents lack effective communication skills. Some are verbal skills, such as asking good questions and making effective statements. Some are skills that lead to good decision making. Each communication skill is made up of simple steps to follow in order to say things in the best possible way. Once these skills are learned, parents' communication with their children will surely improve.

Parents who use good communication skills are, at the same time, teaching their children to use good skills. When parents use angry or hostile words, their children do too. Often parents *cause* the very behaviors they don't want in their children. In short, they "reap what they sow."

Parents with differing ideas about how to parent can all raise children who become successful adults. Some parents are direct and authoritarian, controlling their children's behavior. Some parents allow their children to discover the consequences of their actions with little or no interference. Still other parents have a style between these two where they negotiate with their children. Each of these parenting styles has its own risks, and each can be highly successful in developing a solid adult. This book supports your choice of parenting styles — you can be the parent YOU want to be.

A common mistake of parents is using several parenting styles in similar situations. For example, one time parents make a decision about a child's bedtime and another time they let the child decide. A change in style confuses children and makes them feel less secure. This book, in a practical and insightful way, shows you how to avoid giving your children contradictory or mixed messages. Warmth and consistency can be easily understood by children through something as simple as seeing love in a parent's eyes and hearing a parent's genuine laugh. Any parent can practice and learn the "how-tos" of effective, comfortable, and loving communication, even in challenging situations.

This book was designed so that parents get results in a short period of time. Learning the *12 Communication Skills for Effective Parenting* does require some effort. I'm reminded of practicing my golf swing. Along with my good swings, I make errors. When I do, I look at what I am doing and then practice more. Even while under the pressure of a real game, I often make bad swings. Years ago, I would mumble, curse, beat my club on the ground, become more frustrated and angry, and blow my swings. Human relationships are like that too. We have to be consistent in modeling positive, optimistic behaviors — always attempting to self-correct and improve. Your children will benefit from your attempts to improve your communication, and so will society. Your children will copy your attitudes, new skills, and the ways you make decisions. Love, warmth, and caring lead to love, warmth, and caring.

Gary Page's experience as a minister, teacher, and effective parent shines through the skills he teaches in this book and the stories he tells to illustrate them. He allows us to be the parents we want to be and to learn to effectively communicate with our children.

So — enjoy learning these new skills and becoming an effective communicator as you take pleasure in raising your children, being the best parent you can be.

Joseph Hasenstab, President
Performance Learning Systems

Joseph Hasenstab is the creator of Project TEACH™, a Performance Learning Systems course in communication skills for educators, upon which the skills in this book are based.

ACKNOWLEDGMENTS

Every book is the product of many people's work. This book is no exception. Many people made it possible. Foremost among them is Joe Hasenstab, president of Performance Learning Systems (PLS). Joe created *Project TEACH*™, a professional development course taken by thousands of teachers. The 12 communication skills of *Being the Parent YOU Want to Be* were first brought together in *Project TEACH*™. I thank Joe for his permission to adapt *Project TEACH*™, his willingness to take the risk of publishing this work, and his urging to finish it.

I am also grateful to the hundreds of teachers who told me about the great success they had with the 12 communication skills, not only with their classroom students, but also with their own children at home. Their prompting led me to write this book.

Many others contributed as well. First is my wife Rotraud, who encouraged me not to give up on this project that I started 18 years ago. Talk about patience! She is my lover, best friend, greatest fan, and the mother of Jason and Deidre, my grown children. By their love, patience, and forgiveness when I got it wrong, I am richly blessed. They, and the thousands of children I have taught and counseled during more than 30 years of teaching, have taught me all I know about children.

To my extended family — Carol, Ronnie, Andrew, Michelle, Deborah, and Stephen Weir; Bubby and Zaidy

Greenspoon; "Uncle Phil" and wife Cindy and their children, Cory and Zoey; and Elly (also a Greenspoon) and husband Dan Wolf and their children, Aaron and Sarah — I wish to express my love and appreciation for allowing our family to be bound inextricably to theirs. I am deeply indebted to them, and my own family, for providing me with much of the illustrative material in this book and for giving me permission to use it.

In memoriam, I offer my thanks to my parents, Alice and Neville Page. They set me on my course. Their forbearance and love allowed me to become what I am, even when the becoming often confused and frustrated them.

Further, I wish to express my deep appreciation to all the staff of Performance Learning Systems. Their tireless work has made this book what it is. Without their efforts, especially those of Miriam Georg and Doris Cannady in the PLS office in Texas, Barbara Brown, Cathy Chmel, Donna Burke, and Ardella Koskinen in the PLS office in California, and many other people not known to me, there would be no book at all. I also extend my appreciation to Duane Newcomb and Joanna Robinson for editing and proofreading.

Finally, I thank you, the readers, for purchasing and using this book. I look forward to hearing from you about your experiences with the 12 communication skills. I will derive great satisfaction from your success as you use this book to help your children grow to be responsible, independent adults. God bless you all.

Gary Page

INTRODUCTION

Would you like to have a positive relationship with your children? Do you want to understand them better? Would you like to overcome their reluctance to do what you ask? Or to do the right thing?

Well, that's what this book is all about: becoming the parent *you* choose to be. It will show you how to build a positive, lifelong relationship with your children by using good communication skills — speaking effectively, listening carefully, asking good questions, and being consistent. So if you are already a parent, thinking of becoming a parent, or just curious, this book is for you.

None of us is born a good parent. We must learn. We raise our children mostly by trial and error based on our childhood experience and the experiences of others. The 12 communication skills you will learn are the result of many years of research and practice. They are easy to learn, easy to understand, and easy to use.

As an aid, we will give you lots of practice and suggestions. Each is an important part of *Being the Parent YOU Want to Be*. As you practice them, your communication skills will improve. You will see how they help you deal with your children and their problems almost immediately.

The book begins in Part 1 by helping you find your parenting style. Part 2 gives you four ways to discover what's behind your children's words and actions. Part 3 offers four new communication skills to help manage your children's objections. The remaining four communication skills, found in Part 4, explain how to help your children solve problems and make sound decisions.

Part 5 asks you to role-play — act out roles to practice the 12 skills. The *12 Communication Skills for Effective Parenting* work well when groups of interested parents work together. You can also practice these communication skills with a partner at home. For best results, you should role-play as soon as you read each section and before going on to the next one.

Finally, in Part 6, we bring everything together.

HOW TO USE THIS BOOK

Are you a busy person? Then this is the book for you. We designed it to be read in small parts so that you can practice the parenting skills and make them yours. If you read and practice about 20 minutes a day, you will soon master each of the *12 Communication Skills for Effective Parenting*.

It will take you through simple stages toward being the kind of parent *you* choose to be. It holds a wealth of useful information about managing your children. It guides you with questions and provides activities to help you create the parenting style you want. This book encourages *you* to decide how many activities to try. You will be asked to respond in one of several ways, by:
- Bracketing or checking one or more choices.
- Underlining a word or phrase.
- Filling in a blank. (We suggest that you write your answers on a separate sheet of paper rather than mark or write in this book so that you may share it with others. This is especially important if you are reading a library copy!)

Once in a while you'll do some experiments. At other times you will make observations. Sometimes we will ask you to share your thoughts and ideas with someone else: your spouse, a special friend, or anyone with whom you feel comfortable. Many parents find it's also a good idea to discuss their thoughts and ideas with their children. You decide.

The different practices in this book will help you improve your parenting skills and learn more about yourself and your children. As you learn the *12 Communication Skills for Effective Parenting*:

- You will become a more encouraging parent.
- Your children will become more cooperative.
- You will enjoy being with them more than ever.
- You will feel more relaxed at the end of your busy day.

Summary Boxes

From time to time you will find boxes such as this. They summarize:

- The terms and meanings of the skills taught in *Being the Parent YOU Want to Be*.
- Important steps you will need to remember.

HERE'S HOW

The Here's How section in each box gives examples of how to use the specific skill summarized in that box.

Whenever we ask you a question, we give you the answer immediately after it. If you get stuck, just look at the answer and go on to the next question. For the best results, as you read each question, cover the answer below it with a piece of paper or a bookmark.

To help you move from theory to practice, we have you do some Bridge-Building Activities. Doing them will build your confidence. They will also help you to use the skills naturally and quickly. Do as many of the Bridge-Building Activities as you can.

Now and then, as you work through the book, you will see some things repeated. This helps strengthen your understanding of the skills and ideas. As you do each practice, you can apply your new communication skills in your everyday dealings with your children. As you go along, your skills will improve. You will also see that they are helping your children become responsible, independent adults.

TO SUM UP

Choosing *Being the Parent YOU Want to Be: 12 Communication Skills for Effective Parenting* is the start of a wonderful adventure in successful parenting. By the time you finish this book, you will be using the skills effectively. Soon you *will* be the parent *you* want to be!

Part 1

"My Way, Your Way, or Our Way?"

▶ Discover
Your
Parenting
Style

Have you ever . . .

- thought you might be too hard on your children?

- thought you might be too lenient?

- felt you might make too many decisions for your children?

- considered what kind of parent you would like to be?

This section will address these and many more questions about your parenting style.

1

How Do YOU Parent?

*E*ach mother or father has a different style of parenting. What is yours? Do you tell your children what to do? Do you let your children explore problems on their own? Are you firm and strict because your children need lots of guidance? Are you permissive, letting your children guide themselves?

THREE PARENTING STYLES

There are three distinct parenting styles: "My Way," "Your Way," and "Our Way." Most parents favor one style over the others. Knowing your parenting style — and sticking to it — is important.

"My Way" parents often make all the decisions and want instant obedience from their children. Parents of very young children often find themselves deciding for their children. This approach is called "keeping the power" (for the parent).

"My Way" parents:
- value obedience.
- decide for children.
- usually have young children.

"Your Way" parents are permissive. They demand little of their children. These parents let their children do their own thing as much as possible. Such parents do not control or punish. They often let very young children make decisions. We say this is "giving the power" (to the children).

"Your Way" parents:
- are permissive.
- seldom demand much.
- value children's independence.
- let children decide.
- rarely punish.
- usually have older children.

"Our Way" parents get their authority from their knowledge and experience rather than from their position or power.

"Our Way" parents:
- provide directions.
- are flexible.
- value give-and-take.

These parents "share the power" of decision making with their children. They give clear, firm directions softened by reason and a give-and-take of ideas. As their children mature, these parents often share more of the decision-making power with their children.

Effective parents want to raise responsible, independent children. They seldom use only the "My Way" or the "Your

Way" approach. As their children mature, many parents begin to use more "Our Way" and "Your Way" strategies. Knowing which kind of decision making you use will help you become a more effective parent.

CONSISTENCY AND CONGRUENCY

Two things are necessary for any style of parenting to be effective: consistency and congruency. Consistency means your words and actions must always send the same message to your children. For example, every time your child goes out to play without finishing a chore, you have the child come back and finish it. Each time your child comes home late for supper, the child gets nothing to eat — if that is your rule. "Being consistent" also means doing what one parent we know did. Her son skipped school to go to the beach with his friends. When the school called her, she drove to the beach and, to her son's embarrassment, took him back to school. He didn't skip school again.

To some parents, this may seem harsh. Yet research shows that parents who use words and actions that always send the same message make their children feel more secure than parents who don't. Consistent parents are predictable. Children perform better when they know what to expect. This gives them a feeling of security. It leaves them free to learn more about the world around them. Children of predictable parents are often more sure of themselves and more dependable. They often learn more quickly than children of less predictable parents. I'd recommend you read the book *Child Management: A Program for Parents and Teachers* for its excellent discussion on consistency and predictability (see more details on page 337 in the Bibliography).

Congruency is different from consistency. Being congruent means making sure that your words and body language say the same thing to your child. What you *do* and *how you look* must agree with what you *say*. Suppose, for example, you say to your child, "I'm not angry." If, however, you fold your arms across your chest, raise your voice, and clench your teeth when you say it, you are not being congruent since your words and your actions do not match. You look and sound angry but say you are not.

Your words and actions need to copy your parenting style. If you say you are a "Your Way" parent, your words and actions agree with each other when you let your children decide for themselves. "Do as I say, not as I do" is the opposite of congruency in this case.

Here is an example of what I mean. Suppose you are planning an early morning start for a trip to the zoo. The night before, you worry about whether your children will get enough rest for the long day ahead. You want to make sure they get to bed at a reasonable time. In such a case, you might say something like this:

> Children, we're going to have a long day tomorrow, and you will need lots of rest tonight. I want you to be in bed by 9:00. ("My Way" statement)

If you believe your children are too young or too immature to decide for themselves and you decide for them, you would be congruent. Your decision to have the children go to bed by 9:00 would match your belief that you should decide bedtimes.

On the other hand, you might feel that by talking with your children you could come to a decision you all agree on. You might say something like this:

Children, tomorrow is a big day. You need a good rest tonight so you'll enjoy our trip. Let's decide what time you should be in bed tonight. ("Our Way" statement)

If you believe your children are able to decide for themselves, or if you feel they will learn more from deciding what time to go to bed, you might include your children more in the decision-making process. In such a case, you might say:

We want to feel well rested for all the fun we will have tomorrow. What do you think would be a good time to go to bed tonight? ("Your Way" statement)

Any one of these approaches is acceptable. What matters is that your decision matches your "My Way," "Your Way," or "Our Way" parenting style.

Parents who claim to share decision making ("Our Way"), but give many orders ("My Way"), only confuse their children. When children are confused, they find themselves constantly testing rules to find out which ones you will make them obey, and when. They have little time left to explore and to learn from the world around them.

For example, my neighbor, Mrs. Brown, has a son, Taylor. Mrs. Brown is in the habit of telling Taylor what she wants and what he can expect if she doesn't get it. Unfortunately, when her son doesn't follow the rules, Mrs. Brown doesn't do what she has threatened to do. As a result, Taylor tests every rule, over and over, to see which ones he has to follow. Not making your child follow all of the rules leads to even more testing. This constant testing of rules can sometimes be dangerous. I will show you why.

With my car windows rolled down one hot summer day, I was driving up our street. As I got close to our house, I heard Mrs. Brown call out, "Taylor, don't ride on the road, or I'll take your bike away."

Knowing that Mrs. Brown rarely enforced her rules, I quickly stopped my car. I was certain Taylor would test this rule as surely as he tested every rule Mrs. Brown made. Suddenly, Taylor rode out from behind the garage and into the street in front of my car. If I hadn't stomped on the brakes, I would have hit him. Since Taylor could not be sure which of his mother's rules she really wanted him to follow, he had to test all of them. As a result, Taylor used most of his energy testing rules. He had little time left to explore and to learn from the world around him.

TAYLOR AT HOME

Interestingly, at school, where Taylor had a very predict-able teacher, he rarely tested the rules. At school Taylor knew a rule made was a rule enforced. Feeling safe, he was free to do his classroom work.

TAYLOR AT SCHOOL

Consistency and congruency are critical to effective parenting. Being a consistent "My Way," "Your Way," or "Our Way" parent is far better than being an inconsistent parent, no matter what your style.

Even so, you may be more comfortable with the "My Way" approach while your children are very young, and decide to change first to "Our Way" and then to "Your Way" as they get older. This decision often depends on your cultural background and the way you were brought up.

Also, some researchers have found that many children seem to learn better in an "Our Way" environment. That is why *Being the Parent YOU Want to Be* often emphasizes the "Our Way" skills.

Whether you choose to make the family's decisions or take a more permissive approach, as long as you are consistent and congruent (your words, actions, and body language say the same thing), you *will* increase your chances for success. Consistent, congruent parents are more likely to raise responsible, independent children than are those parents whose words, actions, and body language often disagree.

WHAT IS YOUR PARENTING STYLE?

We are going to do a number of practices and worksheets in this book. To help you find the practice or worksheet you need to do next, we have numbered them within each chapter.

Practice 1

This first practice helps you to know what your present parenting style is. When you have completed the exercise, you will find out whether you prefer the "My Way," the "Your Way," or the "Our Way" approach. You may be surprised to learn that your approach is not what you thought it would be. Remember that if you have young children you will naturally be more authoritarian than parents of mature teens. The reverse is also true. It is also true that wide differences exist among parents of children in any age group.

On Worksheet 1: My Perceived Parenting Style, page 14, mark an X where you think you are now on each of the three scales. Show what percentage of the time you do "My Way," "Your Way," or "Our Way" parenting. The percentages from each column, when added together, should total 100 percent (see the sample worksheet on page 330 in Appendix C).

For example, you may be concerned for your children's safety. They may be very young and lack experience. If so, you may need to give directions most of the time and let them decide only occasionally. You may also decide to give them a few choices at times. If you do that, mark an X near the top of the "My Way" scale and nearer the bottom of the "Your Way" and "Our Way" scales.

On the other hand, your children may be mature teenagers, and you may give them a lot of say in what happens. If so, place your X closer to the top of the "Your Way" scale and lower down the "Our Way" and "My Way" scales.

If you regularly share decisions with your children, mark an X nearer the top of the "Our Way" scale and farther down the "My Way" and "Your Way" scales.

The sample worksheet on page 330 in Appendix C shows just one possible response. In fact, a great number of possibilities exist. Fill out Worksheet 1: My Perceived Parenting Style now.

Worksheet 1
My Perceived Parenting Style

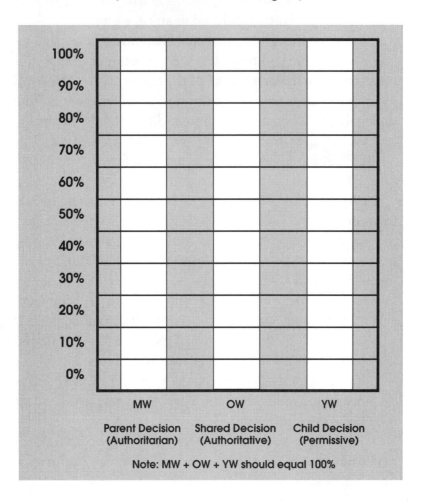

Note: MW + OW + YW should equal 100%

SOME WORDS OF CAUTION
AND ENCOURAGEMENT

Some parents may find their parenting styles aren't what they thought they were. At first this may discourage you. This is especially true if you prefer to control the decision making, rather than share it with your children. Take heart. Just remember, *developing congruency between your actual and your intended parenting style is more important than whether you keep, share, or give decision making to children.*

Ideally, the parenting style you think you use (Worksheet 1) and your *actual* style (Worksheet 4B, which you will do later) are the same. In the end, whether to keep, share, or give decision making to your children is up to you. As you decide, consider this: I have found the most effective parenting takes place when you and your children work *together* as they grow up.

When the parenting style you believe you are using and your actual parenting behavior are not in step, you may begin to feel anxious and grow to resent your children. They also may grow to resent you. For example, Jacob's mother wanted to go to a movie, but she chose to ask Jacob what *he* wanted to do. When he chose miniature golf, she grudgingly went along even though she preferred the movie. They both had an unhappy time because she had given him the decision-making authority that she had really wanted to keep for herself. In fairness to both of them, she should have told Jacob in the very beginning where she would take him.

Wanting to use one parenting style and actually using another parenting style can be stressful. This is especially true if you have a "My Way" style and want to use a "Your Way" or "Our Way" style.

In *Being the Parent YOU Want to Be*, "to make a decision" means to solve problems, settle arguments, or determine outcomes. If you want to develop a style of sharing or giving decision making, you need to learn skills that make sharing and giving decision making possible. If you allow your children to decide, you must be willing to support their decisions. If you have *any* doubts about what their decisions might be, then you decide. It is better to tell your children what to do than to tell them "no" after you have let them decide. If you want them to have some part in the decision-making process, give them a choice of possibilities that you can agree to.

WHO DECIDES?

As a parent, you make most decisions. Household chores need to be done. You also must decide how things will be done and how you intend to enforce the rules. There are times when you may want children to make some of the decisions that affect them. At other times, you will keep decision making. Practice 2 examines the kinds of decisions you will make and those you will share with your children.

Practice 2

For each item on Worksheet 2: Who Decides? on page 17, show the approximate *percentages* of time you:

1. Decide yourself ("My Way").

2. Involve your children in the decision ("Our Way").

3. Allow your children to decide for themselves ("Your Way").

For example, who decides where you will take family vacations? Is it your decision alone? Do your children share in it? Do they decide without your input? A sample answer appears on the worksheet. Complete the worksheet in a similar way. (You may also refer to the completed sample Worksheet 2 on page 331 in Appendix D.)

Worksheet 2
Who Decides?

Next to each statement below, show the percentage of time you:
1) Keep decision-making authority.
2) Share decision-making authority with your children.
3) Give decision-making authority to your children.

When added together, the three columns across each row should total 100%.

Example:
Who decides how to budget the family income?   85%   10%   5%

	MW Parent Decision	OW Shared Decision	YW Child Decision
1. Who decides what you will eat at mealtimes?			
2. Who chooses when and where your family will go for vacation?			
3. Who sets the rules for the way your children act at home?			
4. Who decides what happens when the kids break these rules?			
5. Who decides who will do which chores?			
6. Who picks your children's friends?			
7. Who decides what your family will do on your vacations?			
8. Who chooses your children's clothes and hairstyles?			
9. Who decides by what time your kids have to be home in the evening?			
10. Who sets bedtimes?			
Totals:			

DECISION-MAKING CONTROL

As you use this book, you will become more confident that your children will do the right thing. You may find you share more of the decisions with them, especially as they grow older. Sometimes you may decide to keep, share, or give the power based on your feelings. As important as feelings are, sound judgment should determine what you do rather than let your emotions decide.

Practice 3

Suppose you are planning a vacation for which you can afford to spend up to $2,000. Also, suppose that you can only be away for two weeks. If you want to make the decisions, you might say this:

> PARENT: Children, we're going to Florida for two weeks over the Christmas holidays. We're leaving by plane on December 20, after school is out.

If you want to share the decisions and let your children have a choice, you might say this:

> PARENT: We need to plan our Christmas vacation this year. We have $2,000 set aside for it. This year we have only two weeks, and I don't want to drive very far. So I have chosen some resorts where we can go. All of them have lots for you to do. Which one would you like to go to?

On the other hand, your children may be older, in high school, or about to graduate. If you want to let them decide, you might say the following:

PARENT: I've got good news. Our plant is shutting down over Christmas vacation and I have been given a $2,000 bonus for my sales achievement. We can take a trip together. Where would you like to go with the money we have?

With these choices in mind, complete Worksheet 3: Factors in Decision Making on page 20. (You may also refer to the completed sample worksheet on page 332 in Appendix E.)

Worksheet 3
Factors in Decision Making

Next to each statement below, show the percentage of time you:
1) Keep decision-making authority.
2) Share decision-making authority with your children.
3) Give decision-making authority to your children.

When added together, the three columns across each row should total 100%.

Example:
The making of rules in our home is usally a: 70%   20%   10%

	MW Parent Decision	OW Shared Decision	YW Child Decision
1. My children would like more:			
2. Because of the age and maturity of my children, I tend more toward:			
3. Because of the problems I deal with, I favor:			
4. Because I am concerned about my children, I prefer:			
5. Because I work, or I am short of time, I prefer:			
6. Pressure from others, such as my husband/wife, influences me toward:			
7. The way friends treat their children makes me favor:			
8. How my parents raised me makes me want to use:			
9. If I didn't have to consider anything else, I would choose:			
10. Day-to-day I lean toward:			
Totals:			

Practice 4

There are two more worksheets to complete: 4A: Summary Table for Worksheets 2 and 3, and 4B: My Actual Parenting Style. To find your actual parenting style, use Worksheet 4A on page 22 first. On Worksheet 4A, do the following:

1. Refer to your Worksheet 2: Who Decides? on page 17. Enter the totals from each column of Worksheet 2 in the appropriate spaces going across the page. (These three numbers should total 100 percent.)

2. Now refer to your Worksheet 3: Factors in Decision Making on page 20 and do the same. (These three numbers should also total 100 percent.)

3. Add the two numbers in the MW column and enter the total in the box for these totals. Do the same for the OW and YW columns.

4. Divide each of the totals (gathered in step 3 above) by 2 and enter the answer in the space provided.

5. Now divide each of those totals by 10 and enter the answers in the space provided. These numbers should be written as percentages. (See sample Worksheet 4A on page 333 in Appendix F.)

Take these percentage totals and transfer them to Worksheet 4B on page 23 by marking an X at the appropriate percentage level in each column (MW, OW, and YW). (See sample Worksheet 4B on page 334 in Appendix G.)

Worksheet 4A
Summary Table for Worksheets 2 and 3

	MW Parent Decision (Authoritarian)	OW Shared Decision (Authoritative)	YW Child Decision (Permissive)	Work- sheet Totals
Worksheet 2				
Worksheet 3				
Totals for Worksheets 2 and 3				
Divided by 2				
Divided by 10 (round off to nearest whole number and show as a percentage)				

Worksheet 4B
My Actual Parenting Style

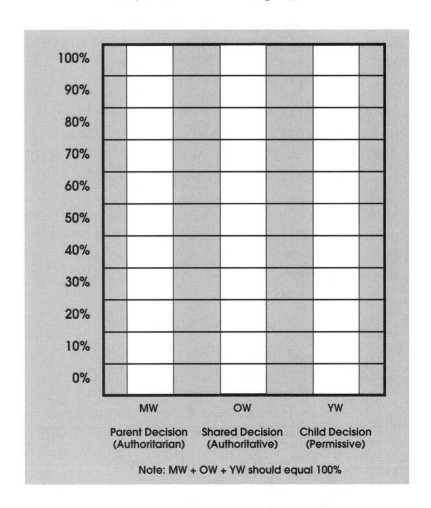

Note: MW + OW + YW should equal 100%

Practice 5

Look at Worksheet 5: Are You Congruent? on page 25. The left three columns are labeled MW ("My Way") at the bottom of the page. The middle three columns are labeled OW ("Our Way"). The three columns on the right are labeled YW ("Your Way"). Do the following:

1. In *each* set (MW, OW, YW), within the columns titled "Perceived Parenting Style" (the style you believe you use), mark Xs where you marked Xs on Worksheet 1: My Perceived Parenting Style.

2. Connect these three Xs with a red line.

3. In *each* set (MW, OW, YW), within the columns titled "Actual Parenting Style," mark Xs where you marked Xs for Worksheet 4B: My Actual Parenting Style.

4. Connect these three Xs with a blue line.

5. For the "Desired Parenting Style" columns, decide the percentages for MW, OW, and YW that you desire your parenting style to be. Then mark your Xs for those percentages. (These three columns should also equal 100 percent.)

6. Connect these three Xs with a green line.

(See the sample Worksheet 5 on page 335 in Appendix H.)

Worksheet 5
Are You Congruent?

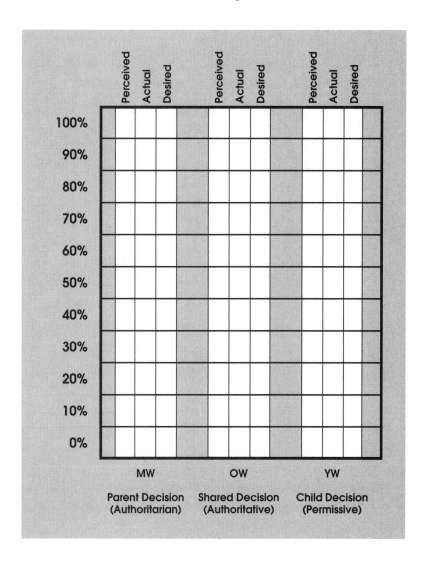

WHERE TO FROM HERE?

You must now decide whether the above results satisfy you. If you find you are not congruent, and don't actually parent the way you would like to, then you need to bring the colored lines for your "Desired Parenting Style" on Worksheet 5 closer together. To do this, you could change how you believe you raise your children or how you actually raise them. You could even decide to change both.

That's up to you. What's important is that you become congruent. If you wish to change, use the style and communication skills you will learn in this book that best express your new ideas of how you want to raise your children. Use more strategies that match your desire to a) keep decision-making control, b) share it, or c) give it to your children.

The decision is yours. As you read the remaining chapters and do the activities and Checkups, you will quickly learn the skills that will help you become the parent you want to be.

Part 2

"What Are You Thinking?"

▶ Discovering
What's On
Your
Child's
Mind

Have you ever . . .

- wondered what was really on your child's mind?

- wished you could understand your child better?

- asked yourself, "What did he or she mean by that?"

- wanted to get your child to rethink what he or she said?

This section will show you how to find out what is on your child's mind.

Researchers tell us that we need to repeat something 20 times to master it. In this book, we offer you many chances to practice each of the 12 skills. In this section, we begin with the first four. These communication skills help you discover what is on your child's mind. Regardless of your parenting style, you will find these skills useful.

***

**Discovering
What's-On-Your-Child's-Mind Skills**
Help parents understand children's:
- Actions
- Feelings
- Viewpoints
- Intentions

***

Children have their own ways of doing things that make sense to them, and usually have good reasons for doing what they do. Those reasons we call children's intentions. The more you understand your children's *intentions*, the easier it will be for you to work with them. While intentions may be confirmed, they are not facts because they have not yet been realized or carried out. Knowing children's intentions (what's on their minds), you can encourage positive change. Four **communication skills** will help you uncover what's on your children's minds and help you deal with them.

2

"Are You Thinking . . . ?"

*Tell-Me-What's-On-Your-Mind
Question (TWM) and
Give-Me-Specific-Information
Question (GSI)*

**Tell-Me-What's-On-Your-Mind
Question**

- Gives children the freedom to speak.
- Addresses what *they* think is important.
Is often used with a "Your Way"
parenting style.

Here's How

1. "What do you think we should do
   with the stuff in the attic?"
2. "How did you choose Camp Sequoia?"

Tell-Me-What's-On-Your-Mind Questions let your
children speak freely. They allow children to tell you what is
on their minds. Tell-Me-What's-On-Your-Mind Questions help

children tell you what *they* consider important. For example, here are three Tell-Me-What's-On-Your-Mind Questions:

PARENT 1: What do you think?
PARENT 2: How did you decide?
PARENT 3: Why are you so upset?

Give-Me-Specific-Information Question

- Limits children's answers to "Yes" or "No" or
- Requests only what you want to know.
Is often used with a "My Way" parenting style.

Here's How

1. "Are you going to the prom?"
2. "Do you have any homework?"
3. "Which picture do you like better?"

The Give-Me-Specific-Information Question *limits the answer a child can make.* If asked in one way, the Give-Me-Specific-Information Question may call for a "Yes" or "No" response, as in the following examples:

PARENT 1: Will you be staying for basketball practice?
PARENT 2: Have you finished your homework?
PARENT 3: Will you help me paint the bedroom?

Give-Me-Specific-Information Questions can also ask for exactly what you, as a parent, want to know:

> PARENT 1: How are you going to complete your paper route today?
>
> PARENT 2: When are you going to take out the garbage?
>
> PARENT 3: Whose turn is it to set the table?

"My Way" parents use mostly Give-Me-Specific-Information Questions; "Your Way" parents prefer Tell-Me-What's-On-Your-Mind Questions; "Our Way" parents freely use either.

Practice 1

Now try the following practice exercise: Circle whether a question below is a Tell-Me-What's-On-Your-Mind Question (TWM) or a Give-Me-Specific-Information Question (GSI). Remember to cover the answers at the end until you finish working through the exercise.

a. "What do you think will happen now?"
TWM   GSI

b. "Did you see that show about Africa on television last night?"
TWM   GSI

c. "What choices do we have?"
TWM   GSI

d. "What time are you supposed to be home?"
TWM   GSI

e. "Whose turn is it to clear the table?"
TWM   GSI

f. "How do you feel about that?"
   TWM   GSI

Answers:
a. TWM, b. GSI, c. TWM, d. GSI, e. GSI, f. TWM

Below you will see another series of questions. In the blank, write either TWM for "Tell-Me-What's-On-Your-Mind" or GSI for "Give-Me-Specific-Information." Again, cover the answers until you have finished.

PARENT: What were you thinking? _____

PARENT: When do you think you will have your room cleaned? _____

PARENT: How did you decide that? _____

PARENT: What will you do to have your project ready by Monday? _____

Answers:
TWM, GSI, TWM, TWM

As you can see, the Tell-Me-What's-On-Your-Mind Question gives children a chance to speak freely. With Tell-Me-What's-On-Your-Mind Questions, children can tell you what they mean. What they believe is important may surprise you!

Practice 2
In the spaces below, write three Tell-Me-What's-On-Your-Mind Questions you might ask your children. Cover the examples given below until you have finished.

1. _____
_____

2. _____
_____

3. _____
_____

Possible Answers:
Any questions that let your children speak freely.
For instance:
"How might you have avoided the problem?"
"What theme could we have for your party?"
"When would you like to take out the trash?"

In the spaces below, write four Give-Me-Specific-Information Questions you might ask your children that could be answered with "yes" or "no."

1. _____
_____

2. _____
_____

3. _____
_____

4. _____
_____

Possible Answers:
"Is Simone going with you?"
"Have you finished your homework?"
"Are you going to look for a job this weekend?"

Next, write three Give-Me-Specific-Information Questions that ask for a specific piece of information.

1. _____
   _____
2. _____
   _____
3. _____
   _____

Possible Answers:
Any questions that tell you what you want to know:
"When will you be home?"
"How are you getting to the game?"
"Whose turn is it to feed the dog?"

Both Tell-Me-What's-On-Your-Mind Questions and Give-Me-Specific-Information Questions help you talk with your children and work out problems with them. Now let's see *how* you can use Tell-Me-What's-On-Your-Mind and Give-Me-Specific-Information Questions. First we will look at examples of how to use each communication skill, then we will see how some parents do it.

The issue of control is the difference between the two communication skills. With a series of Give-Me-Specific-Information Questions, there is *more parent control* of the child's answers. The answers to Give-Me-Specific-Information Questions lead to what a parent really wants to know — what's on the child's mind.

On the other hand, there is *less parent control* with Tell-Me-What's-On-Your-Mind Questions. Such questions let children *explain* why they did something and give you more information. Also, Tell-Me-What's-On-Your-Mind Questions take more time to answer, allowing both parent and child to think more carefully about their replies.

When you are trying to help your children think, look at different ways of doing things, explain themselves, and use reason, Tell-Me-What's-On-Your-Mind Questions are best. They give free rein to your children's imagination, creativity, and judgment.

In the following exchange, we see how asking a series of Tell-Me-What's-On-Your-Mind Questions (TWM) can help your child see a range of possibilities while helping you understand what he or she is thinking. You can end the series of Tell-Me-What's-On-Your-Mind Questions with a Give-Me-Specific-Information Question (GSI) that helps your child draw the right conclusion from the answers he or she has already given.

PARENT: How do you feel, Donna? (TWM)

DONNA: I'm still upset about being cut from the hockey squad.

PARENT: What can you do to change that? (TWM)

DONNA: Nothing. The roster is already posted.

PARENT: What other sports would you like to participate in? (TWM)

DONNA: I really like hockey.

PARENT: What other activities do you like? (TWM)

DONNA: I like swimming, but that's not till summer. Baseball starts soon, though.

PARENT: Will you wait for summer or try baseball now? (GSI)

DONNA: I'll try baseball.

DONNA'S DILEMMA

Asking a series of Tell-Me-What's-On-Your-Mind Questions works best when children have the facts they need. Whenever your child does *not* reply to a Tell-Me-What's-On-Your-Mind Question, or when you want to get a particular answer, use Give-Me-Specific-Information Questions. You may even use a *series* of Give-Me-Specific-Information Questions to limit the *kind* of answer your child can make and quickly get the response *you* want. The following conversation uses a series of Give-Me-Specific-Information Questions:

> PARENT: Are you still upset about being dropped from the hockey team? (GSI)
>
> DONNA: Sure, wouldn't you be?
>
> PARENT: Yes, I would be. Baseball starts soon. Are you eligible to try out? (GSI)
>
> DONNA: Yes.

PARENT: Will you? (GSI)

DONNA: Yes.

When used properly, Give-Me-Specific-Information Questions can lead your child to an expected decision. Be careful, though. Avoid using a heavy-handed series of Give-Me-Specific-Information Questions that say, "Now I've got you." Doing so only creates resentment.

In the next example, a parent has just discovered his child copying homework answers from a classmate's notebook. Compare the following two ways in which the parent could handle this problem:

PARENT: Do you think it's a good idea to use your friend's homework answers? (GSI)

CHILD: I guess not.

PARENT: Do you think that using someone else's work helps you learn the material? (GSI)

CHILD: No.

PARENT: Will it help you pass your test? (GSI)

CHILD: No.

PARENT: Will it help you get a passing grade? (GSI)

CHILD: No.

PARENT: Then what will you do to learn what you need to get a passing grade? (GSI — or TWM if the parent really wants to know what the child thinks)

CHILD: I guess I better get some help.

This parent closed every possible door through which the child might have backed out. The child had no choice. She had to decide that it wouldn't do her any good to use another student's homework. This approach, however, is pretty heavy-handed. While the child gets the point, he or she can feel boxed in and resentful. Children hate to admit that their parents are right and they are wrong.

Questioning does not have to be tough. In fact, by using a balance of good Tell-Me-What's-On-Your-Mind *and* Give-Me-Specific-Information Questions, you will help your children think through their problems. In the final example, the parent uses a series of Tell-Me-What's-On-Your-Mind and Give-Me-Specific-Information Questions to help his daughter think. See how the Give-Me-Specific-Information Questions lead the child to the important points and give her the clues she needs to answer the final Tell-Me-What's-On-Your-Mind Question.

PARENT: Are you using Yolanda's notes? (GSI)

CHILD: I can't do it myself.

PARENT: What makes it hard for you? (TWM)

CHILD: Some of the stuff I just forgot . . . and some I don't understand at all.

PARENT: How did you decide to use the material from Yolanda's book? (TWM)

CHILD: I have to have this stuff done for tomorrow. If it's not done, Mrs. Brown will kill me! Yolanda's good at math. She always gets the answers right. I knew she'd lend me her book.

PARENT: Will copying Yolanda's work help you to understand it? (GSI)

CHILD: No, I guess not.

PARENT: What would help you understand it now? (TWM)

CHILD: I guess I could ask for help.

PARENT: Who might help you? (TWM)

CHILD: Yolanda knows how to do it . . . and my teacher will help if I ask. But I have to have this done for tomorrow! I can't wait.

PARENT: Who could help you now? (GSI if the
          parent has an answer in mind. Otherwise,
          it's a TWM.)

CHILD: Would you help me?

The above way of asking questions makes it easier for the child to talk and gives the parent time to listen for what the child has in mind. It also helps both parent and child solve the problem without arguing or losing face.

Tell-Me-What's-On-Your-Mind and Give-Me-Specific-Information Questions, then, used by themselves or in combination with each other, can help you and your child talk more easily about any subject.

CAUGHT IN THE ACT

WATCH THE WAY YOU SAY IT

Before you go on to the next skill, take a few moments to consider *how* to ask questions. Let's eavesdrop on a parent as she asks the same questions in two different ways:

PARENT: How did you tear your jeans, Megan?

MEGAN'S JEANS
SCENE 1

Compare that question to the same parent's question below. As you read it, place the emphasis on the words in bold type.

PARENT: How did you **tear** your **jeans**, Megan?

MEGAN'S JEANS
SCENE 2

Do you hear the differences? In fact, the two questions are very different. While the words were the same in each case, *how* the parent said them was not. *What* you say to children is often less important than *how* you say it. The "how" is in your tone of voice.

In Part 1 of this book, we used the term "congruency" (see page 7). As you read on, you will see why your words and your body language (nonverbal signals) need to send the same message. You will learn how your facial expressions, the words you emphasize, the way you stand, and the way you use your hands affect your messages to your children.

Recall the parent asking Megan about the tear in her jeans. Remember in each example that the words the parent used were the same. It was the tone of voice that was different. In the first example, the mother's tone was neutral, indicating a sincere desire to know how Megan had torn her jeans. With no trace of accusation, her voice sounded genuine and positive, and was therefore effective. She was *congruent* because *what* she said matched *how* she said it.

In the second example, the mother's emphasis on the words "tear" and "jeans" suggested that she was critical of Megan for tearing her jeans, possibly even angry. In fact, the emphasis turned the question into a statement: "You were careless to tear your jeans." Had the mother made that statement directly, she would have been *congruent* because her words would have matched her tone and her genuine feelings. Megan would have known exactly what her mother was thinking, with no possibility of confusion.

Some questions make statements. Such questions do have their place in discussions with your child. You must know, though, whether or not your questions *do* make statements. You need to listen carefully to yourself. The way you phrase your questions, the tone of voice you use, the words you emphasize, and your body language all influence the messages you convey to your children.

Read the following questions aloud. Can you hear the different message each conveys?

PARENT: **Haven't** you **finished** the dishes?

Compare that to:

PARENT: Have you finished the dishes?

How are these questions different?

Notice that the first parent used "haven't," while the second parent used "have." "Have" is positive; "haven't" is negative. The use of "haven't" implies, "You should have by now." Using "have" is a better, more positive way of asking. A positive approach will usually meet with less defiance. (Of course, depending upon the parent's tone of voice, the second way could also say sarcastically: "You know, I'm waiting for you to finish.")

The second question is easier for the child to answer because it is a sincere request for information, not a veiled statement. When you ask your child a question to which you already know the answer, it is important to be aware that quite often the question is really a statement. You may, however, make good use of such a question as long as you are doing so intentionally. Asking questions that make statements can be effective if you:

1. Avoid sarcasm.

2. Use a questioning tone.

3. State your questions positively.

4. Use body language that is congruent (agrees with your words).

CHECKUP

The checkups in this book are not tests. They are meant to help you learn the *12 Communication Skills for Effective Parenting.* Feel free to look at the correct answers that are listed after the checkup whenever you wish.

There are two types of questions, _____

_____ and _____

_____. Tell-Me-What's-On-Your-Mind Questions

give children _____ to speak,

and tell parents _____.

Give-Me-Specific-Information Questions limit children's answers

to _____ or _____, or focus on a _____

_____.

Sometimes parents ask questions to which they already know

the answers. They ask these questions in order to avoid the

potential _____ that direct statements may

bring out. These questions-that-make-statements can be very

effective provided parents: avoid _____, use a

_____ tone, phrase questions _____,

and use body language that is _____.

Possible Answers:
Tell-Me-What's-On-Your-Mind, Give-Me-Specific-Information, maximum freedom, what is important to the child, "Yes," "No," specific piece of information, hostility, sarcasm, questioning, positively, congruent

3

"Did I Hear You Right?"

What-You-Meant Statement (WYM)

*O*ur third skill is the What-You-Meant Statement, which enables you to better understand your child's feelings, attitudes, or intentions (what your child really means). The What-You-Meant Statement is an empathetic way of looking at what your child says; it shows that you care about what he or she thinks and brings out the real meaning of your child's words and actions.

What-You-Meant
Statement

Step 1. Think positively.
Step 2. Make a verbal statement.
- Restate the child's meaning and
- Offer that meaning back to the child.

This is a "Your Way" parenting approach.

Here's How

1. "You're angry about failing the course." (*feeling*)
2. "You'll put the tools away when you're finished." (*intention*)
3. "It doesn't matter which flavor you have." (*attitude*)

The What-You-Meant Statement focuses on one of two possibilities: 1) what the child actually said, or 2) what the child intended to say. For example, suppose a child says the following to you:

CHILD: I didn't make my bed this morning because I had to get to school.

Here are two What-You-Meant Statements a parent might make in response:

PARENT: You didn't have enough time to make your bed. (Clarifies a *fact*.)

PARENT: You wanted to make your bed before leaving for school. (Clarifies what the child intended to do.)

VALIDATION

The "fact" you clarify may be your child's *feelings* about what happened, such as being called names at school:

CHILD: I hate it when the kids at school tease me.
PARENT: It hurts when people make fun of you.

You can also bring out your child's *attitude* or *belief*:

CHILD: Making the drinking age 21 is stupid. I can vote when I'm 18.
PARENT: If you can vote, you should be able to drink.

Notice in this example that the parent's What-You-Meant Statement gives a clearer meaning to what the child believes. Notice, too, that the parent made the point less passionately. This not only clarifies children's thinking, but also tones down the intense feelings that children, like their parents, sometimes have.

To sum up, the What-You-Meant Statement helps you understand what your child's words or actions mean to them. When you understand your children better, you will find it is much easier to talk to them, and they will appreciate being understood.

Practice 1

With this in mind, do the following: After each statement below, use a What-You-Meant Statement to say what you believe the child means. You are just confirming facts. Think of three different facts to confirm. Here is the first:

> CHILD: I didn't know I had to come right home after school.

What-You-Meant Statement:

1. _____
   _____
2. _____
   _____
3. _____
   _____

Possible Answers:
"You thought you could come home any time."
"You didn't understand the rule about coming home
   after school."
"You felt free to come home when you were ready."

Here is another:

CHILD: I couldn't finish my homework.

What-You-Meant Statement:

1. _____
   _____
2. _____
   _____
3. _____
   _____

Possible Answers:
"It was too hard."
"You didn't have enough time."
"You got too tired to finish last night."
"You had too much else to do today."

Not only can the What-You-Meant Statement confirm a fact, but it may also bring out what the child intends to do. The following is an example of a parent using the What-You-Meant Statement to clarify what the child has only *suggested* he or she will do:

CHILD: I didn't think he'd be so mad when I hid his boots.
PARENT: Then you won't be hiding them again.

The What-You-Meant Statement can also bring a blurry meaning into focus or redirect that meaning into something the parent wants the child to do.

CHILD: I guess I will have to take better care of my stuff.

PARENT: From now on you'll put your things away after you use them.

Practice 2

Read the following statements. In the spaces provided, write the suggested or expressed intentions that might underlie what the child says:

CHILD: I didn't mean to spill paint on the floor.

What-You-Meant Statement:

1. _____
   _____
2. _____
   _____
3. _____
   _____

Possible Answers:
"You'll be cleaning it up."
"You'll be more careful next time."

Here's the last example:

CHILD: I'll remember to bring in my bike.

What-You-Meant Statement:

1. _____
   _____

2. _____
   _____
3. _____
   _____

Possible Answers:
"It will be put away tonight."
"You want to keep it safe."
"You'll put it away when you're finished."

Practice 3

A What-You-Meant Statement can also confirm your child's feelings. In the spaces provided, write a What-You-Meant Statement you might make to check on a child's feelings. (See Feeling Words on page 329 in Appendix B.)

CHILD: I can't finish my homework.

What-You-Meant Statement:

1. _____
   _____
2. _____
   _____
3. _____
   _____

Possible Answers:
"You are frustrated."
"The homework is boring to you."
"You feel incapable of doing it."

CHECKUP

Complete the blanks:

The _____

helps make the meaning of your child's words or actions much

clearer. What-You-Meant Statements respond to _____

(including _____ and _____ the

child has), or suggested or expressed _____.

As you understand your children better, you will be able to talk

more _____ with them.

Answers:
What-You-Meant Statement, facts, feelings, attitudes,
intentions, positively

Notice that while "intentions" can be checked, they are
not "facts" because they have not been carried out yet.

4

"Everybody Does It!"

Think-It-Over Statement (TIO)

*W*hile the What-You-Meant Statement helps you understand your children better, the Think-It-Over Statement helps *your children* understand *themselves*. It's a way of getting them to consider an opinion or an action.

Think-It-Over Statement

Step 1. Mentally identify the part of your child's thinking that doesn't make sense.

Step 2. Restate that part of your child's position that doesn't make sense.

This is an "Our Way" parenting approach.

Here's How

1. "You believe you can go over
   the entire course the night before
   the exam."
2. "You expected to get in even though
   you aren't old enough."
3. "All the judges were against you."

Sometimes children say things that are not logical, such as the statement "Everybody does it." Often different parts of their statements and opinions don't agree with each other. If children realize this, they might change their thinking. The Think-It-Over Statement is useful to help your children see their mistakes when they're not being logical.

Here are two examples:

BOY: Why can't I come home whenever I feel like it? All my friends do. They get to stay out as late as they want.

PARENT: All the other kids get to stay out no matter how late.

Another example:

GIRL: I don't like Bobby. He's stupid. He can't even catch a baseball.

PARENT: You only like good baseball players.

Sometimes parents find that their children really believe ideas that seem illogical. When this happens, parents can give their children more information that will often help to change their minds.

IDEAS FOR JUSTIN

Practice 1

The following is a Think-It-Over Statement:

> JUSTIN: I'm going to drop out of school and get a job.
> PARENT: You believe you can get a good job without a
>   high school diploma.

The above Think-It-Over Statement requires two steps. Write the Numbers 1 and 2 in front of two statements that are the first and second steps of the Think-It-Over Statement.

_____   Mentally identify what makes sense in the
          child's statement.

_____   Pick out what does not make sense in the
          child's statement.

_____   Say in another way what does not make sense
          in the child's statement.

Answers:

Pick out what does not make sense in the child's statement.
  Say in another way what does not make sense in the
  child's statement.

An important feature of the Think-It-Over Statement is
that you say it in the same matter-of-fact voice as the What-
You-Meant Statement. Otherwise, it's not a true Think-It-Over
Statement. For example:

CHILD: Taking money off the counter wasn't so bad.
          It was only 75 cents.

PARENT: *(sarcastically)* You think it's **honest** to take
          even a small amount of money.

Compare that to the following response without the
emphasis on the word "honest."

PARENT: *(calmly and in a near monotone, emphasizing
          no words)* You think it's all right to take a
          small amount of money that isn't yours.

People have a greater stake in changes that they decide
on for themselves, rather than changes others decide on for
them. A good Think-It-Over Statement lets children see what's
wrong with their thinking. If stated in an aggressive or
sarcastic tone, it tells children that their ideas are stupid or

silly. The Think-It-Over Statement should always give children a chance to take a second look at their ideas or beliefs so they can change their minds if they want to.

When using Think-It-Over Statements, you must avoid saying or suggesting, "Aha, I've got you." If children sense you are gloating, they will feel manipulated or tricked, and they may become resentful. Both your body language and your tone of voice can give this feeling to your child. So listen carefully to your child's response, watch his or her body language, and let your words and actions agree with each other. Don't let your words, tone of voice, or actions imply that you won and they lost.

Practice 2

For practice, write your own Think-It-Over Statements in response to each of the following children:

> CHILD: I don't want to wear my rain boots. The other kids don't.

1. _____
   _____
2. _____
   _____
3. _____
   _____

Possible Answers:
"You'd rather risk a cold."
"You'd rather look good to your friends than stay healthy."
"It's okay if your shoes get wet."

Here is another child:

CHILD: I only said that so *I* wouldn't get into trouble. (Tattled on innocent brother.)

1. _____
   _____
2. _____
   _____
3. _____
   _____

Possible Answers:
"Telling a lie will keep you out of trouble."
"You won't get into trouble when you blame the problem on someone else."
"He won't mind you saying that he did it."

Now, another child:

CHILD: Why should I practice my drums if I can't take any more lessons till next fall?

1. _____
   _____
2. _____
   _____
3. _____
   _____

Possible Answers:
"You'll remember everything over the summer."
"Getting ready for lessons is the only reason to practice your drums."
"You'll get better without practice."

I want to make one final point before leaving this section: Many parents feel they can change their children's minds more easily by asking questions. Read the following child's question and the parent's reply.

DISHES SCENE 1

BOY: Why should I do the dishes? That's
          girls' work.
MOTHER: Shouldn't both girls and boys do
          household chores?

Compare the mother's question to the following Think-
It-Over Statement:

MOTHER: (*calmly and in a near monotone, emphasizing
          no words*) You believe that only girls should
          do household chores.

What are the differences between the question and the statement? The first mother uses a Give-Me-Specific-Information Question to imply that the child *ought* to believe that both men and women can do housework. She also suggests that something is wrong if her son doesn't agree with her. Her son will likely be defensive, even hostile. Children, like adults, are more likely to change when *they* decide to, rather than when a parent tells them to. A good Think-It-Over Statement points out what's wrong so children can see for themselves.

CHECKUP

Fill in the blanks:

To review, the Think-It-Over Statement is a way of getting a child to look at _____ with what he or she said. The first step of the Think-It-Over Statement is to _____ _____ the part of the child's thinking that doesn't make sense. The second step is to _____ the child's position to include _____.

Possible Answers:
what's wrong, mentally identify, restate,
what doesn't make sense

5

What Have You Learned?

This chapter asks you to practice the four communication skills you have learned so far by responding to some situations that involve parents and children. Each situation contains brief discussions between parents and children that will help you learn *when* and *how* to use the skills.

Practice 1

In the following examples you will identify the skills we have covered so far:

1. Tell-Me-What's-On-Your-Mind Questions (TWM)

2. Give-Me-Specific-Information Questions (GSI)

3. What-You-Meant Statements (WYM)

4. Think-It-Over Statements (TIO)

Background Information
Parent: Mr. Harris
Child: Jennifer

Jennifer is an intelligent child who has a good relationship with her father, Mr. Harris. However, Jennifer tends to be bossy and argumentative with her playmates. Her continual quarreling, punching, and shouting at other children often get Jennifer into trouble, and she has very few friends. Jennifer is now playing in the backyard alone, and Mr. Harris

takes the opportunity to speak with her. He hopes to find out why Jennifer argues so much and to help her change the way she acts.

Read along as Mr. Harris talks with Jennifer. Identify the skills Mr. Harris uses in the spaces provided. (Cover the answers until you have identified the skills.)

MR. HARRIS: Jennifer, how many arguments have you been in this week?

Name the skill: _____

Answer:
Give-Me-Specific-Information Question

JENNIFER: I don't know.
MR. HARRIS: I'd say at least three, wouldn't you?

Name the skill: _____

Answer:
Give-Me-Specific-Information Question

JENNIFER: Yeah . . . I guess so.
MR. HARRIS: How come?

Name the skill: _____

Answer:
Tell-Me-What's-On-Your-Mind Question

JENNIFER: They won't play with me, and if I try to
               join their games, they start calling me
               names. They always want to fight.

MR. HARRIS: I see. It's always their fault.

Name the skill: _____

Answer:
Think-It-Over Statement

Jennifer chooses to ignore the incongruity in her own remarks, giving instead another reason for her fighting:

JENNIFER: Nobody likes being called names. It
               makes me mad.

MR. HARRIS: *(calmly)* When you get angry, the only
               thing you can do is punch someone.

Name the skill: _____

Answer:
Think-It-Over Statement

Jennifer recognizes she isn't making sense, yet refuses to accept what she is doing:

JENNIFER: I'm not gonna walk away and let them
               make fun of me.

MR. HARRIS: You feel you have to do something.

Name the skill: _____

Answer:
What-You-Meant Statement

Jennifer thinks for a moment, then continues:

JENNIFER:	At least when I hit them they stop calling me names.
MR. HARRIS:	They stop for good.

Name the skill: _____

Answer:
Think-It-Over Statement

JENNIFER:	Well . . . yeah!
MR. HARRIS:	Why do you think they want to call you names, Jennifer?

Name the skill: _____

Answer:
Tell-Me-What's-On-Your-Mind Question

JENNIFER:	They hate me, Daddy. They don't want me to play with them.
MR. HARRIS:	*(calmly)* Everyone at school hates you and never wants to play with you.

Name the skill: _____

Answer:
Think-It-Over Statement

> JENNIFER: It feels that way.
> MR. HARRIS: Could you be doing something they
>   don't like?

Name the skill: _____

Answer:
Give-Me-Specific-Information Question

> JENNIFER: Like what?
> MR. HARRIS: I wonder, Jennifer. Could it be that you
>   order the kids around? Sometimes you
>   yell at your little brother and order him
>   around. Then what does he do?

Name the skill: _____

Answer:
Give-Me-Specific-Information Question

> JENNIFER: *(reluctantly)* He gets mad and calls me
>   terrible names.
> MR. HARRIS: Just like the kids at school.

Name the skill: _____

Answer:
What-You-Meant Statement

JENNIFER: Yeah . . . I guess so.

MR. HARRIS: Jennifer, has bossing the other kids
               around gained you many friends? Has it
               stopped their teasing?

Name the skill: _____

Answer:
Give-Me-Specific-Information Question

This direct Give-Me-Specific-Information Question
draws an admission from Jennifer:

JENNIFER: No, they keep doing it, and nobody will
               play with me.

This time Mr. Harris ignores the part about *nobody* playing with Jennifer. Instead, he focuses on the fact that being
bossy does not help her get and keep friends:

MR. HARRIS: So, being bossy hasn't helped. What do
               you think *might* help?

Name the skill: _____

Answer:
Tell-Me-What's-On-Your-Mind Question

The Tell-Me-What's-On-Your-Mind Question that follows
the Give-Me-Specific-Information Question makes Jennifer
consider other ways to act:

JENNIFER: Maybe I could try doing what they
             want sometimes.
MR. HARRIS: Do you think they would enjoy your
             company more?

Name the skill: _____

Answer:
Give-Me-Specific-Information Question

JENNIFER: Yeah . . . maybe . . . but I don't know . . .
             Then we'd always do what they want,
             and I wouldn't get to do what I want.
MR. HARRIS: Doing what you want is worth the
             hassles of fighting and the loss of
             having friends.

Name the skill: _____

Answer:
Think-It-Over Statement

This response produces the desired effect:

JENNIFER: No. I'm always getting into trouble . . .
             and the kids don't like to play with me.
MR. HARRIS: Yes. Wouldn't you like to stay out of
             trouble and have more friends?

Name the skill: _____

Answer:
Give-Me-Specific-Information Question

This pointed Give-Me-Specific-Information Question gets the desired response from Jennifer again:

JENNIFER: We'd probably fight less.
MR. HARRIS: And if the kids fight with you less often, they are more likely to do what you want to do.

Name the skill: _____

Answer:
What-You-Meant Statement

JENNIFER: Yeah . . . I guess so.
MR. HARRIS: So, what are you going to do?

Name the skill: _____

Answer:
Tell-Me-What's-On-Your-Mind Question

JENNIFER: I'm going to do what they want to do sometimes.

Mr. Harris looked for Jennifer's intentions and then responded to them. All the while, he kept to his own plan and let her see what she could do to solve her own problem.

Practice 2

In this activity you will make up examples of the communication skills we have learned:

  1. Tell-Me-What's-On-Your-Mind Questions (TWM)

  2. Give-Me-Specific-Information Questions (GSI)

  3. What-You-Meant Statements (WYM)

  4. Think-It-Over Statements (TIO)

Background Information
Parent: Mrs. Jimenez
Child: Arturo (10 years old)

Arturo dislikes most of his studies (especially reading and spelling), although he can easily do them. Dinner is over and Arturo goes into his room to study his spelling words for tomorrow's test. When Mrs. Jimenez checks on him, he is organizing his baseball cards. She talks to him, hoping to make Arturo realize that learning his spelling words comes before sorting his baseball cards.

In the spaces below, write out a sentence using the communication skills required. Write it as you might actually say it to Arturo. Remember that the way you express each communication skill may be different from the answers provided. There are many possible responses, and the suggested answers are given as models to help you.

Start with a What-You-Meant Statement to let Arturo know that Mrs. Jimenez sees him playing with his baseball cards rather than studying his spelling.

_____

_____

BASEBALL CARDS VS. SPELLING

Possible Answers:
"You are sorting your baseball cards."
"You have decided to do your spelling later."

Asking a Give-Me-Specific-Information Question, clarifying that Arturo is doing something other than spelling, would also be correct when used with a neutral tone of voice. An example would be: "Have you finished your homework?"

Mrs. Jimenez begins by asking a Tell-Me-What's-On-Your-Mind Question:

MRS. JIMENEZ: Arturo, how did you decide to sort your
              baseball cards instead of doing your
              spelling now?

ARTURO: Oh . . . er, we're going to trade them
              first thing tomorrow morning. I don't
              want to trade any of my singles.

Phrase a Think-It-Over Statement Mrs. Jimenez might use to point out the incongruity here.

_____

_____

Possible Answers:
"It's okay to sort your cards first when you have a spelling
   test tomorrow."
"You've decided this is more important than spelling."

Mrs. Jimenez's Think-It-Over Statement might go like this as the discussion continues:

MRS. JIMENEZ: You believe you can get your spelling
              done in time for the test tomorrow and
              organize your cards too.

ARTURO: I need to get my cards sorted. Kendra
              and I are trading tomorrow. I'll get my
              spelling done.

Arturo recognizes the incongruity of his position. Nevertheless, he feels the time pressure makes it more important for him to finish sorting his cards than to do his spelling. Phrase a Think-It-Over Statement that would help him to change his mind.

_____

_____

Possible Answers:
"Sorting your cards is more urgent than the spelling test."
"You thought you could do both your card sorting *and*
    your spelling."
"You think you can get both done before going to bed."

The talk continues with Mrs. Jimenez giving a Think-It-Over Statement:

MRS. JIMENEZ: Sorting your cards now is more
               important than finishing your spelling
               assignment on time.

ARTURO: I guess not . . . but I have to get it done!
               I'm not going to be ready to trade to-
               morrow if I don't.

Write a Think-It-Over Statement that might help Arturo in his dilemma.

_____

_____

Possible Answers:
"Being ready to trade your cards is more important than
    being ready for the spelling test."
"The test is less important than trading your cards."

Mrs. Jimenez's response reveals Arturo's faulty thinking and allows him to consider other options:

MRS. JIMENEZ: You can trade your cards with Kendra only tomorrow morning.

ARTURO: Well, no. We could trade at lunch time or at recess. But Kendra and I plan to meet before class to trade.

Ask a Tell-Me-What's-On-Your-Mind Question that would help Arturo think about doing his spelling words first. Your Tell-Me-What's-On-Your-Mind Question must also lead him to keep his promise to Kendra.

_____

_____

Possible Answers:
"What are you going to do?"
"How can you get your spelling done and still trade with Kendra tomorrow?"

Arturo can now reply:

ARTURO: I guess . . . by doing spelling now. I can call Kendra and ask her if we can trade cards at lunch.

Use a What-You-Meant Statement to suggest Arturo's implied intention:

_____

_____

Possible Answers:
"You'll put away your cards now."
"You'll study spelling now and sort your cards later."

Let's see how Mrs. Jimenez handles the situation with a What-You-Meant Statement:

MRS. JIMENEZ: Then you won't sort your cards until after you finish your homework, and you'll call Kendra to set a new time.

Let's leave Mrs. Jimenez and Arturo now and see how some other parents use these communication skills *in real-life situations*. They did it, so can you!

THEY DID IT, SO CAN YOU!

The problems parents face at home are like those teachers handle at school. As a teacher, I once stopped two boys who were running down the hall playing tag.

"Boys!" I called out. "How are you supposed to go down the hall?" (Give-Me-Specific-Information Question — because the answer was known)

"Walk, sir," they replied in unison.

"What are you going to do, then?" (Give-Me-Specific-Information Question)

"Walk."

Immediately they walked down the hall, ducked outside, and finished their game of tag.

Kids can hardly wait to grow up. The teacher caught our eight-year-old daughter, Deidre, and a friend smoking in the school washroom and called us. Soon after Deidre arrived home, I asked her about it:

"You had a problem at school today. (What-You-Meant Statement) Do you want to tell me about it?" (Give-Me-Specific-Information Question)

Immediately tears filled her eyes. "I was smoking."

"Why were you smoking?" I asked. (Tell-Me-What's-On-Your-Mind Question)

"I don't know," she said, as the tears kept coming.

"You're very upset." (What-You-Meant Statement) I wanted her to know I understood how she was feeling.

"Yes!"

"What should we do about this?" (Tell-Me-What's-On-Your-Mind Question)

"I don't know." Deidre was calming down a little. The tears dried up.

"I don't want you to smoke," I continued. "Smoking is not good for you. I love you and want you to be healthy. If you keep smoking, you might make yourself sick."

"I'm sorry, Daddy."

"Does that mean you won't smoke anymore?" (Give-Me-Specific-Information Question) At this point I felt she might agree to stop smoking.

"I only smoked because Jennifer did."

Clearly, I had tried to get a commitment too soon.

"It was Jennifer's fault you were smoking." (Think-It-Over Statement)

"No," she replied sheepishly.

"You made up your own mind to smoke." (What-You-Meant Statement)

"Yes." Deidre realized she was responsible for her own actions.

"What will you do next time a friend asks you to smoke?" (Tell-Me-What's-On-Your-Mind Question)

Smiling, Deidre looked straight at me and replied proudly, "I'll say, 'No way.'"

"Then," I confirmed, "I can be sure you won't smoke anymore." (What-You-Meant Statement)

Entirely at ease now, Deidre said, "I promise, Daddy."

"Let's go make supper," I added as I hugged her, and off we went.

Sometimes parents are too quick to force *their* way of doing things on children. Often it is better to help children think through a problem themselves. For example, a single parent we know seldom let his children settle their own troubles. They would always bicker and fight until he put a stop to it. After taking one of my seminars, this single father tried a different way.

While traveling down the expressway in the back seat of the family car, his children began to argue loudly.

"What's going on back there?" (Tell-Me-What's-On-Your-Mind Question)

No answer.

"Are you two fighting?" (Give-Me-Specific-Information Question)

Again, there was no answer, just more bickering.

The father remembered what he had learned about ignoring negative behavior whenever possible. He said nothing to the children as they went on fighting for several more minutes.

Finally his daughter called out from the back seat: "Daddy, aren't you going to stop us?"

"I know you can settle it yourselves." (What-You-Meant Statement)

The children stopped fighting.

This example clearly shows that parents do not always need to get involved. Children don't need a referee to settle their differences. In fact, parents may sometimes make matters worse. As the proverb says, "Sometimes it's better to sit still than rise to fall."

The simple, everyday conversations we have with our children present excellent opportunities to encourage them. Asking Tell-Me-What's-On-Your-Mind Questions can do that.

While visiting a friend, I overheard this conversation:

"Hi, Cory! How was school today? Did you have fun?" Mother asked.

"Yup," he replied cheerfully.

"What did you do today?"

"We played." He seemed a little impatient that his mother didn't already know that.

"What did you like best?"

"The math center."

After a few moments, he added, "I like the playhouse . . . blocks, too . . . and that's all."

"Tell me, what do you learn when you play at school?" Mother asked.

"No fighting and no dogs allowed!" Cory said loudly.

His mother and I could hardly keep from laughing, but Cory was so serious about it that we didn't say another word.

Soon Cory continued, "We make sets and patterns. We count, too . . . with the blocks. Sometimes we just build stuff."

"Like what?"

"Big buildings."

"What else do you learn?"

"Not to make noise . . . how to play nice. And we learn to take turns and share stuff."

"When I was in your classroom over the summer," his mother said, "I saw lots of books. What do you do with the books?"

"Just read them. What else would I do with books?"

His mother could hardly keep from laughing.

"I already read ten of them. I practiced," Cory said.

"Whom do you like to play with?"

"I like to play with Koryn." He paused, then added, "I just like her."

His mother smiled. "How high can you count now?"

"A hundred!" And he did it.

"What do you want to learn at school tomorrow?"

"To be good." Cory ended the conversation as he gulped down the milk and cookies his mother put out for him.

Many problems parents deal with at home start at school. One of my workshop parents faced such a problem. One day her daughter Deepa arrived home, threw her school bag on the floor, and stomped into the room.

"I hate Mrs. Mendez! She's such a witch!"

Her mother turned and calmly confirmed Deepa's feelings: "You are mad at Mrs. Mendez." (What-You-Meant Statement)

DEEPA IS ANGRY

"You know what she did? She canceled the class trip because two of the boys were fighting in class. That's not fair. Nobody else was fighting. Why should everybody be punished because of them? She's stupid."

Again her mother spoke quietly: "Just because two boys fight, you don't think everybody else should have to miss the trip." (What-You-Meant Statement)

"Yeah!" Deepa said in a quieter voice. "Why should the rest of us miss the trip? It just isn't fair."

"It sounds like you're upset about missing the class trip and don't know what to do about it." (What-You-Meant Statement)

"What can I do? Teachers do whatever they want. Nobody cares what *we* think."

"There's nothing you can do," said Mother, trying to point out what was wrong with Deepa's thinking. (Think-It-Over Statement)

Deepa was now much calmer and ready to take another look at the problem.

"Well, I guess I could talk to her, but she's not going to change her mind. What's the use?"

"You don't think Mrs. Mendez will listen to you, so it's not worth even trying to talk to her." (Think-It-Over Statement)

Deepa's mother knew what Deepa seemed to miss — that Deepa had nothing to lose by trying. Mrs. Mendez might just listen to a good student like Deepa. Besides, Mrs. Mendez had had time to think about it. She might welcome the chance to talk it over.

"I'm just a kid, Mom. She's not going to change her mind because I ask her to."

Deepa still did not seem to understand. So Mother said, "It's not worth trying because she might not change her mind." (Think-It-Over Statement)

"Why should she?"

"You can't think of any reason she would change her mind." (What-You-Meant Statement)

"Well, it was just those two boys. The rest of the class has been working hard to go on the trip. I guess I could tell her I think it's unfair that we all suffer because of them, but she won't listen."

"You don't think Mrs. Mendez knows that most of you have worked hard for the trip. (What-You-Meant Statement) I have a feeling she may be fairer than you think." Deepa's mother knew Mrs. Mendez was a reasonable person.

"I could try, I guess. But I know it won't do any good."

"Are you going to try?" Mother asked. (Give-Me-Specific-Information Question)

"She might listen."

"You've got nothing to lose, have you?" (What-You-Meant Statement)

"I guess not."

"Let me know what happens," Mother added and left the room.

Deepa did talk to Mrs. Mendez. After thinking about it awhile, she decided the class could go. The two boys, however, had to stay behind. By listening actively and allowing Deepa to work through the problem with her own thinking, her mother helped Deepa to become a more responsible, independent young woman.

Sometimes children need help in understanding that they must face the consequences of their own actions.

"Can I use your gloves, Dad?" Darren pleaded. The snow was falling lightly after a storm the night before, and Darren was excited about building his first snowman of the season in the woods behind the family's house.

"You want to build a snowman, but you came outside without your mittens," his father said calmly. (What-You-Meant Statement)

"I didn't want you and Melissa to start without me," Darren replied.

DARREN FEELS the RESULTS

"Getting here rapidly was more important to you than having mittens to keep your hands warm." (Think-It-Over Statement)

"Yeah, I guess so." Darren stumbled for words. He'd gotten the point.

"What are you going to do?" his father asked. (Give-Me-Specific-Information Question)

"I'll go and get them right now," he said excitedly, and off he went.

"We'll wait until you get back. Hurry!"

Soon Darren was back, his hands tucked warmly inside his mittens.

TO SUM UP

The four communication skills in this section help you — and your child — find out what's going on in your child's mind. They will also help both of you focus on what your child actually means as you talk together. In the next section, we will introduce four more communication skills that will help you encourage your child to change his or her mind. As you master these four new communication skills, you will find it a lot easier to deal with your child.

BRIDGE BUILDING

Try this. Take 30 minutes or so to sit and just listen to your children. This could be a special time you set aside just for listening, but I suggest instead that you just listen to them when you are doing things together: having dinner, playing a game, or going for a walk. They will talk to you when the time is right, and when they do, give them your undivided attention. Why? Parents spend lots of time talking *at* their children when their children do something wrong. We all need to learn to talk to our kids in depth when nothing is wrong. We also need to listen to our children more often. How else will we really get to know them? How will we know what they think and feel? How else will we learn what is important to *them*?

As your children talk, clarify what they say. Their reactions to your statements will give you a clearer idea of what your children mean. Avoid offering advice, adding your own view, or being critical. If you are confused or need more information, ask questions to help you understand. Use Tell-Me-What's-On-Your-Mind Questions to give your children room to respond in their own way. Give-Me-Specific-Information Questions, while easier to ask (and perhaps that's why parents ask so many), limit how children can answer.

Use Think-It-Over Statements sparingly. While they can play a part in problem solving, they don't work well if you use them all the time.

This is a time to really hear what is on your child's mind. How thoughtful he or she really is may surprise you. Listening often brings you closer together. Sometimes children only need a parent's undivided attention. When you listen carefully, they feel respected and valued. So enjoy this time together. You'll be glad you did.

After you listen, you might want to reread Part 2: "What Are You Thinking?" — Discovering What's On Your Child's Mind. This will help you be able to use the skills naturally and automatically.

PRACTICE ROLE-PLAYS

On page 273 you will find role-plays that allow you to practice the skills of this section. Practicing with other adults before using the skills with children is helpful to many people.

LET'S TAKE A BREAK

Before reading on, you might take a week to practice these skills so they become second nature to you. Then come back and learn more.

Part 3

"I Don't Want To!"

▶ Overcoming
Your
Child's
Objections

Have you ever . . .

- wished you could take back what you said?

- been too critical of your child?

- wondered how you could truly understand what your child feels?

- asked yourself, "How can I help my child think more clearly?"

- considered how you might encourage your child to keep trying when threatened by failure?

This section will show you how to be more supportive of your child and overcome his or her objections to your requests.

INTRODUCTION

The four communication skills you will learn in this section will help your children see your point of view and give them more confidence in themselves. All four communication skills will gain your children's cooperation without harming their often fragile egos. They will also help you and your children see eye-to-eye most of the time.

Why is this important? In parent-child relations, positive is better! Fortunately, there is something good in every problem. For example, children who cheat on exams want to pass, and those who steal must plan carefully to get what they want. A parent's challenge is to change negative actions into positive ones.

Many parents have trouble with the issue of stealing. Feelings against stealing run high. Yet a child who steals *does* show attributes that we might otherwise praise. Looking for these attributes and pointing them out to the child have proven effective in redirecting the child's behavior into constructive activities. Children who steal are often lacking attention or feeling unloved. When stealing or other serious problems become chronic, a good therapist should be sought.

Seeing the "up" side of "down" situations often requires quite a bit of creative thinking on the parent's part. Unfortunately, many parents get discouraged and overreact to their children's mistakes. For the long-term well-being of yourself and your children, you must think positively and focus on what your children do right. When parents stress their children's good points, the children's learning and behavior often improve.

Now let's look at our four new communication skills: Look-On-The-Bright-Side Statements, Walk-In-Their-Shoes Statements, Catch-Them-Doing-It-Right Statements, and Support-Their-Thinking Statements. All of these skills will be useful to you regardless of your parenting style.

6

"Accentuate the Positive . . ."

Look-On-The-Bright-Side Statement (LOBS)

*O*ptimism pays big dividends! Think about those things you enjoy doing. Why do you look forward to doing them? Why do you enjoy others less? Usually we dislike activities we do poorly, while doing something well creates the desire to work harder.

If you keep feeling you are doing poorly at something, you will soon give up trying to do it. Likewise, if others keep telling you how terrible you are at doing it, you will soon move on to something else. Your children often respond in the same way. Do they continue playing games they nearly always lose? No, they want to win — at least sometimes. Like us, children enjoy doing what they do well. While rising to a challenge can be an exciting learning experience, children must see results. They must also feel they have achieved something. No one wants to fail all the time.

Using Look-On-The-Bright-Side Statements, you concentrate on what's right in your children's thinking. The focus is on *should* rather than on *should not*, on *right* rather than on *wrong*. Stress *can* rather than *cannot*, and *do* rather than *don't*.

It is looking at a glass as half full rather than half empty, and then filling it up.

The Look-On-The-Bright-Side Statement is an important part of all parenting skills. It always focuses on the "up" side of a situation.

Look-On-The-Bright-Side Statement

Step 1. Think positively!
Step 2. Tell children what you want
them to know or do.
This is a technique for all parenting styles.

Here's How

1. "Walk when you are carrying
sharp objects."
2. "Use only the peanut butter and
jelly to make sandwiches."
3. "You can come to the table when
you've washed your hands."

Look closely at the first step. This is a mental step. Thinking positively — or looking on the bright side — means concentrating on the good parts of any situation. There are always good parts, even in the worst situations.

The first step, then, in a Look-On-The-Bright-Side Statement is in your mind — *think positively!* The second is to tell your children exactly what you expect from them. When parents point out only what is wrong, or what *not* to do, they leave out the part that tells children what they *should* do. Telling a football player "Don't fumble" does not teach him or her how to make a successful catch. How much better to say, "Hold on to the ball tightly and tuck it into your body."

Instead of telling children, "Don't run in the grocery store!" try "Walk, please." Then they will know what you *do* want done.

A Look-On-The-Bright-Side Statement recognizes what children are already doing that's right. That's a big step toward raising successful children.

Here is an example of one parent's use of Look-On-The-Bright-Side Statements. Mrs. Brown's children are stomping loudly down their apartment hallway. She speaks to them quietly and firmly: "Jon and Martha, walk quietly down the corridor, please." With these words, Mrs. Brown reminds her children of what to do and avoids calling attention to what *not* to do. She stresses the good behavior she expects from them and lets them know they were otherwise doing fine.

Practice 1

After each of the following statements, circle whether it is positive or negative:

    a. "Stop arguing, or there will be no television for you tonight."
       positive   negative

    b. "When you are quiet, I'll start the video."
       positive   negative

    c. "Don't reach across the table like that."
       positive   negative

d. "Ask for what you would like to eat and it will be passed to you."
positive   negative

e. "No! That's not the right wrench."
positive   negative

f. "That's the box wrench. The adjustable wrench is on the workbench."
positive   negative

g. "You've got six out of ten correct."
positive   negative

Answers:
a. negative, b. positive, c. negative, d. positive, e. negative, f. positive, g. positive

As with the other communication skills in this book, your tone of voice and your body language are important if you want to encourage your children to do the right thing. When talking with children, use a positive tone and body language that is in step with your words.

What does a positive tone sound like? Usually the sound of a positive voice is heard in its loudness, pitch, inflection, and rate. A voice with positive loudness would be soft to moderately high without blaring. A positive rate of speech would be moderately fast but not rapid. Positive inflection would either put no emphasis on words or it would put emphasis on words that would cause a child to respond positively. And a positive pitch would be moderately high but not shrill.

What does positive body language look like? When making motions with your hands and arms toward a child, gesture with your palm up rather than pointing with your finger. Keep your arms at your sides, rather than crossing them over your chest. Look directly into a child's eyes, rather than looking away. Frowning, jutting out the chin, raising eyebrows, and sneering are all negative facial expressions that may be replaced with a smile or a pleasant expression.

We "talk" Look-On-The-Bright-Side Statements with our positive voices *and* our positive body language.

Say the following parents' replies out loud and notice the difference between them. One parent is using a Look-On-The-Bright-Side Statement. How is that different from the negative parent's message?

PARENT: (*sarcastically*) **That's** a tidy bedroom!
PARENT: That's a **tidy** bedroom.

The first parent's mocking tone implies that the child didn't even try. The second parent is proud and positive about what the child did.

Compare the following two examples, in which both parents use a positive tone of voice, but differ in their choice of words:

PARENT: That's not right. Shoes don't go on the steps.
PARENT: Shoes go on the rack.

The second parent used Look-On-The-Bright-Side phrasing that stresses the positive and what the child is to do. We see that both our *words* and our *tone of voice* change the meaning of the messages we send our children.

Practice 2

Reword the following four parent statements to Look-On-The-Bright-Side phrasing:

PARENT: That's the wrong jacket to wear tonight! It's cold. Couldn't you figure that out?

Possible Answers:
"The blue jacket will keep you warmer."
"Just a reminder, you should be wearing your warmer jacket tonight."
"Everyone going tonight will be wearing a warm jacket."

PARENT: Stop that shouting!

Possible Answers:
"Talk quietly, please."
"Please keep your voice down."
"Softly, please."

PARENT: You'll never find the socks you need in such a messy drawer.

Possible Answers:
"You will find your socks if you straighten up the drawer."
"Please tidy up your dresser so you can find your clothes more easily."
"If you organize your drawer, you'll find your socks."

PARENT: Arthur, if you don't make better grades, you're going to fail.

Possible Answers:
"With a little more work, you can pass the course."
"You're doing very well in some areas. With a little more effort, you'll get a passing grade. Would you like me to help you?"
"You can get a passing grade if you get your marks up."

CHECKUP

The first step of Look-On-The-Bright-Side Statements is _____

_____. The second step is to focus on

_____

when you speak to them.

Possible Answers:
to think positively, what you want your children to know
or do

EMPHASIZE THE POSITIVE

Later in the book you will learn other communication skills for dealing with problem behaviors. Let me emphasize that using Look-On-The-Bright-Side Statements increases your chances of creating the behavior you want from your children. It is simply a matter of "accentuating the positive," as the song goes.

Compare the following examples:

JOHN: Mom, I'm home.

MOM: You didn't wipe your feet. Look at the mess you've made. Take your boots off and clean it up.

JOHN: Mom, I'm home.

MOM: Hi, sweetheart. Welcome home. (Hugs John.) Now, what can we do about this mud?

MUDDY BOOTS

Clearly, the second mom looked at the glass half full rather than half empty. She avoided using "didn't." John was happy to be home and she was glad to see him. She realized the floor could wait. Welcoming John was her first priority.

Notice, too, how she raised the subject of the floor. She waited, then asked John what could be done about the mess. She let John decide how to get the problem solved. She trusted him to take responsibility for the mess — and she told him so without criticizing. She "accentuated the positive and eliminated the negative."

CAN I GO?

Now let's consider another example:

LYDIA: Dad, Justin asked me to go with him to the game. Can I go?

DAD: Yes, but don't be home late. You can't keep track of time lately. I don't want a repeat of last Saturday night. If you're late this time, you're grounded.

Wow, that was negative! Here's how this father could have handled the situation in a positive way:

LYDIA: Dad, Justin asked me to go with him to the game. Can I go?

DAD: Yes. Remember our discussion last Saturday. Please be home by 11:00. Let me know when you get home. Have fun!

With Look-On-The-Bright-Side Statements, this father is more likely to get Lydia's cooperation. Although he reminds Lydia that she was late last Saturday, he does so constructively. He makes it clear that he wants her home on time this Saturday. He tells her what he wants her to do, not what he doesn't want her to do. What's more, he encourages her to enjoy herself. If you were Lydia, which approach would make you want to do what your dad asked?

"You Feel . . ."

Walk-In-Their-Shoes Statement (WITS)

$\mathcal{S}$uccessful parents are able to see the world from their children's point of view. They let their children know that they understand. This process is called *empathy*. Research shows that parents who show children that they understand and believe in them have fewer conflicts with their children. Their children also feel better about themselves and achieve more at school.

Keep in mind that *empathy* is different from *sympathy*. When you sympathize with children, you feel the same way they do. If they are feeling angry or unhappy, you may try to talk them out of their feeling to avoid the negativity. When you empathize, however, you simply recognize your children's feelings without sharing them. You do not try to change their feelings, but allow your children the right to feel exactly the way they feel. By doing so, you show them that you do understand them.

Imagine for a moment that nine-year-old Mary has just made the following complaint about her brother:

MARY: Jeffrey's taken my bike. Wait till I get hold of him. I'll kill him! He's always taking my stuff. I just hate him!

When some parents hear comments like Mary's they want to say, "You don't really hate your brother. Hurting Jeffrey is wrong and won't solve anything."

Unfortunately, by making statements like these that deny children the right to have their own feelings, parents also suggest that they do not understand those feelings, and conflict may result.

There is a better way. The Walk-In-Their-Shoes Statement is a communication skill that helps you to *empathize* with your children. It recognizes that children's feelings are acceptable even if their behavior is not. It also helps you to make sure you know what your children's feelings really are.

Walk-In-Their-Shoes Statement

Step 1. Let your children know you recognize and empathize with their feelings. Show them that you understand. Perhaps talk about your own or another person's experience.

Step 2. Refocus the child's attention:
a. On a past or future success.
b. In another direction.

This is another "Our Way" parenting approach.

Here's How

1. "It's disappointing to be cut from the school team. Little League starts today." (*empathy followed by a focus in another direction*)
2. "I see you're upset about your bike. You can ride mine until yours is fixed." (*empathy followed by a focus in another direction*)
3. "You seem frustrated. Learning to paint takes time. You'll get the hang of it like you did with drawing." (*empathy followed by a reference to a past success*)
4. "You are really angry about Jane using your idea for the talent show. I know you will come up with something new that will be just as good." (*empathy followed by a reference to a future success*)

Practice 1

In the Walk-In-Their-Shoes Statement below, underline the part that *empathizes* with or understands the child's feelings:

PARENT: Yes, learning to tie your shoelaces can be upsetting at your age. You'll soon learn to tie them. You've learned to button your buttons.

Answer:
Yes, learning to tie shoelaces can be upsetting at your age.

Now consider another Walk-In-Their-Shoes Statement. This time, underline that part of the statement that refocuses the child's attention:

PARENT: It's disappointing not to be chosen as a cheer-leader. In high school I had my heart set on making the baseball team, and they cut me. I was upset too. A person as athletic as you could try out for one of the sports teams.

Answer:
A person as athletic as you could try out for one of the sports teams.

Notice that the second step of the Walk-In-Their-Shoes Statement may take one of two directions. Below, check the two directions you can take in refocusing the child's attention:

    ____   Pointing out the child's problems.
    ____   Pointing to the child's past or future success.
    ____   Discouraging the child from meeting
                 a challenge.
    ____   Telling the child to forget the problem.
    ____   Leading the child in another direction.

Answers:
Pointing to the child's past or future success. Leading the child in another direction.

To sum up, the Walk-In-Their-Shoes Statement improves communications between you and your children. It lets you understand the true *feelings* behind their words or actions. Use the Walk-In-Their-Shoes Statement whenever you deal with children acting out — or acting from — their feelings. The Walk-In-Their-Shoes Statement says that your children's feelings are okay even if their behavior is not. With the Walk-In-Their-Shoes Statement, you help your children change problems into positive experiences. This helps them feel good about themselves and enhances their self-esteem.

CHECKUP

The Walk-In-Their-Shoes Statement is useful when dealing with children's _____ or _____. It recognizes that their feelings are _____ even if their _____ is not. The first step of the Walk-In-Their-Shoes Statement is to _____. The second step is to _____ the child's attention by pointing to either a _____ or _____. You may also lead the child in a _____.

Possible Answers:
feelings, emotions, acceptable, behavior, empathize with the child (with similar examples perhaps), refocus, past or future success, different direction

Practice 2

Now construct some Walk-In-Their-Shoes Statements of your own. For each of the following children's problems, phrase two Walk-In-Their-Shoes Statements. One should point to past or future success. The other should lead the child in another direction.

In this situation, your child can't finger well enough to play a musical instrument.

Past or Future Success: _____

_____

Another Direction: _____

_____

Possible Answers:

Past Success: "I know this is a struggle for you now. Remember how it felt to type on the computer at first? You mastered it with practice."

Future Success: "Fingering can feel strange at first. I'm certain that as you continue to practice, you'll improve."

Another Direction: "Fingering the keys can be awkward at first. You have such good tone and rhythm. What about singing with the children's choir?"

In the next situation, your four-year-old's painting has not turned out the way he expected.

Past or Future Success: _____

_____

Another Direction: _____

_____

Possible Answers:

Past Success: "You are really unhappy. You've done so many great pictures already. Draw another one."

Future Success: "You are angry. Why don't you draw another. It might be your best one yet."

Another Direction: "You must be disappointed. How about helping me make a cake for dessert?"

Finally, a child's model airplane won't fly well after she worked very hard to make it.

Past or Future Success: _____

_____

Another Direction: _____

_____

Possible Answers:

Past Success: "That's upsetting. You've done so well with your models in the past. Some changes to this one could bring better results."

Future Success: "Too bad about your model. The next one could be your best one yet."

Another Direction: "That's frustrating. Let's go over the plans again. We've had some problems before and solved them together."

UNDERSTANDING THE DIFFERENCE BETWEEN FEELINGS AND THOUGHTS

Quite commonly, children believe they are using feeling words when they are not. Similarly, parents sometimes think they are expressing their feelings when they are not. To use the Walk-In-Their-Shoes Statement well, you must separate your true *feelings* from your thoughts about feelings. For example, consider this statement:

CHILD: I feel you're being unfair.

Although the child used the word "feel," he or she didn't express a feeling. In fact, what the child voiced was an *idea* or *thought,* rather than a true feeling.

What children's body language tells us is often different from what their words say. Listen carefully to what your children say, but also pay attention to how they look. Focus, too, on what they do. For example, suppose you are talking to your child and your child says, "I'm listening." When you look at the child's body language you see arms folded across the chest and eyes on the ground. Closed arms are often used to close others out. They say, "You are not welcome. Keep out." Eyes that aren't meeting yours may suggest the child's attention is elsewhere and perhaps you are being ignored. The child says he or she is listening, but the child's body language suggests otherwise.

TWO-STEP CHECK FOR FEELINGS

The following simple tests can help you decide which your child's words express: a true feeling or a thought.

First ask, "Can I insert the word 'that' after the word 'feel'?" If the answer is "Yes," and the message still makes sense, the words describe a *thought,* not a feeling. For example, compare these two statements:

CHILD: I feel this music is boring.
PARENT: You feel (that) this music is boring.

Notice that by adding "that," the message still makes sense. Therefore the child is stating a *thought*, not a feeling.

If the message changes or no longer makes sense when placing "that" after the word "feel" in a statement, the child is describing a *feeling*. For example:

CHILD: I feel lonely today.
PARENT: You feel (that) lonely today.

The insertion of "that" makes the parent message sound nonsensical. From that simple test, we know the child expressed a true feeling.

Practice 3

Which of the following expresses real feelings?

_____   I feel disappointed I can't go.
_____   You feel she should share hers with you.
_____   Mark feels you can do it yourself.
_____   Father and I feel angry when you do that.

Answers:
I feel disappointed I can't go. Father and I feel angry when you do that.

On the other hand, if you can substitute the word "think" for the word "feel," you are also expressing a thought. For example, compare the following:

CHILD: I feel Mark is old enough to baby-sit.
PARENT: You (think) Mark is old enough to baby-sit.

Since the meaning remains unchanged by using "think" instead of "feel," the child is expressing a *thought* rather than a feeling. When the word "think" changes the message or makes it nonsensical, the child is stating a *feeling*. Compare these two statements:

CHILD: I feel angry.
PARENT: You (think) angry.

"Think" makes the message sound nonsensical. Therefore, the child is expressing a true feeling.

Practice 4

In each of the following examples, decide whether the speaker uses "feel" to describe a true feeling or a thought.

PARENT: Some parents feel helpless to do anything about their children's demands.
DOCTOR: I feel parents should never express anger.
CHILD: I feel worn out after a game like that.
CHILD: I feel you haven't done your share of the work.

Answers:
feeling, thought, feeling, thought

Notice that each of these examples had the word "feel" in it. In using the Walk-In-Their-Shoes Statement, many parents start their statement with "You feel . . ." because they know they need to reply to their children's feelings. Until you are comfortable with the Walk-In-Their-Shoes Statement, you might start this way yourself, especially if you find using the Two-Step Check for Feelings easier. Before long, using Walk-In-Their-Shoes Statements will become automatic. You will be seeing the world from your child's point of view and will no longer start your Walk-In-Their-Shoes Statements with "You feel . . ."

To help you learn this skill, you can use the "You feel . . ." method when you practice. Once you learn to use the Walk-In-Their-Shoes Statement, you can use it to support what your child feels.

Practice 5

This next exercise will give you practice in identifying feelings. First read each of the brief statements, then answer them using "You feel . . ." followed by the word that you believe best describes the speaker's feelings. Using the words "You feel . . ." identify *only* what each speaker *feels*.

COLLEGE
STUDENT: I can't believe it! First I win the election, then the scholarship, and now this.

Possible Answer:
"You feel proud."

This time a crying child demands:

CHILD: Gimme the puzzle! Daddy . . . I want the puzzle. I had it first and she took it away.

Possible Answer:
"You feel angry she took your puzzle. If you let her help, she may be able to find the pieces you can't."

Remember: *Show children that what they feel is okay with you, then lead them in another direction.*
This time a neighbor's teenager says:

TEEN: Your children are lucky, Mrs. Goodfellow. My parents are always on my back. They want to

know everything I do. They treat me like I
was a baby.

Possible Answer:
"You feel babied by your parents. Many young people do.
Your parents are used to you being a child and are just
learning to treat you as an adult."

Though we all know many feeling words, we usually
use only a few in talking to others. To help overcome this
problem, I have put together a list of some common feeling
words. You will find the list in Appendix B on page 329.

DEALING WITH ANGER AND OTHER EMOTIONS

One feeling deserves special attention: Anger. Anger is an
intense emotion with many faces. When you sense your child
is angry, look closer. Anger often hides deeper emotions.
Children who lash out in anger are frequently feeling hurt,
disappointed, or rejected. Young children often show their
anger quickly, but hide it as they grow older. Similarly, we
may hide a whole range of feelings or emotions that we have
trouble putting into words.

What feeling does this parent express?

PARENT: I try to be a good mother, but nothing
works. Each day is a running battle. I don't
know where it will end.

Possible Answers:
discouragement, hopelessness, frustration

Consider how this teenager feels:

TEEN: What's the matter with me? All the other
         girls have dates. I don't get invited anywhere.
         Nobody even knows I'm alive.

Possible Answers:
lonely, disappointed, rejected

Here's another:

CHILD: I hate Michael. He never lets me play. He
         thinks I can't do anything.

Possible Answers:
disappointed, ignored, left out, stupid

Practice 6
Read what the child says below. Develop a complete Walk-
In-Their-Shoes Statement that lets her know you recognize
her feelings, then shift her attention.

CHILD: Daddy, I can do it! I don't need your help.
         I'm old enough to fix it myself.

_____

_____

Possible Answer:
"You feel *upset* that I tried to help. You'll be *happier* if you
   do it yourself."

Try this experiment. Clasp your hands quickly, inter-
locking your fingers. Now unlock your fingers quickly and
clasp your hands the opposite way, with your other thumb

on top. Note how awkward and unusual that feels. There is no medical explanation as to why we clasp our hands one way or another — we do so through habit. When we do it differently, it feels awkward. The same is true of the Walk-In-Their-Shoes Statement. It's not a natural way of answering, and it does not fit easily into a typical family conversation.

As with any new skill, the Walk-In-Their-Shoes Statement becomes more comfortable as you practice. Although awkward at first, skiing, golfing, handwriting, and other activities all become easier and more natural with practice. Letting your children know you understand their point of view takes practice too.

Parents must make clear that they are trying to understand their children's feelings. Simply saying, "I know how you feel" doesn't work. You don't know exactly how another person feels. You must check it out!

Look at the next example, in which parents tell a child that they are separating:

CHILD: You and Dad are splitting up? What will I
          do? Don't you care about me anymore?

A suitable Walk-In-Their-Shoes Statement might sound like this:

PARENT: You're worried that you'll be left alone if we
          get divorced. Is that right? Remember, we
          both love you and we'll both look after you.

Use the phrase "Is that right?" when making a Walk-In-Their-Shoes Statement only if you want to. Each Walk-In-Their-Shoes Statement you use may sound strange at first, since it is simply giving your idea of how your child *might* feel. Your Walk-In-Their-Shoes Statements don't tell children how they *must* feel. Even if a Walk-In-Their-Shoes Statement is incorrect, you are still inviting your children to tell you how they do feel. The Walk-In-Their-Shoes Statement is especially useful when responding to an angry child. For example, consider what you would do if this were your child entering your home:

CHILD: What a stupid lunch you gave me! You know I hate carrot sticks. Why can't I have pudding like the other kids? If you give me any more carrot sticks, I won't eat 'em.

For many parents, the natural response to this child would be to come out swinging, at least verbally. Yet when parents shout at children, children stop listening. What is more, parents set an example children are sure to follow. Their children learn how *not* to communicate, and neither parents nor children get what they want. On the other hand, children are more willing to listen when their parents first recognize the true feelings behind what their children say. Then the parents may overcome their children's objections. Consider this parent's handling of the situation:

PARENT: You're upset that I gave you carrot sticks. What else might I give you that will be nutritious?

See the difference? This parent not only showed he or she understood what the child meant — the parent also avoided further escalation of the child's feelings. Both parent and child will have time to cool down and discuss the issue calmly. You must continually practice seeing the child's point of view and recognizing his or her feelings. Regularly ask yourself, "What is my child feeling right now, and about what?" Doing so works!

SUPPORT CHILDREN'S FEELINGS

Let's turn now to some of the other points of the Walk-In-Their-Shoes Statement. Children often go to their parents with problems, but are hesitant at first to risk saying what they really feel. They may test the parent first. In doing so, children are really asking, "Do you care about me? Do you want to help me?" Unfortunately, parents often cut their children off by offering advice too soon. They may even assume responsibility for their children's problems. The real problems may never get talked about.

For example, children who ask a parent's opinion about another child's actions may be worrying about their *own* actions. They might also be trying to find out if the parent cares enough to listen and show concern. The Walk-In-Their-Shoes Statement invites children to continue talking. It encourages them to explain what they really mean.

The secret of the Walk-In-Their-Shoes Statement is first to listen to what the child says, then to sum up what the child means in a way that empathizes with the child.

Let's look at how a poorly handled situation might be managed more effectively using Walk-In-Their Shoes Statements. Look at the first dialogue between Martha and her parent on the next page, then decide how you might have handled the problem differently. Compare what you would have done to the second dialogue, page 128.

MARTHA IS DISAPPOINTED

MARTHA: That stupid Heather! She always messes up.
We could have won our game today if she
hadn't screwed up.

PARENT: Don't talk about Heather that way. It's not
nice. I'm sure she did her best. Besides,
winning isn't everything.

MARTHA: This was an important game. She's such a
dope! (*With that, Martha stomped out of
the room.*)

If you were Martha, do you think you would have felt
any better? Would you have felt your parent understood your
frustration or cared about how you really felt? Not likely. In
fact, you might even be angry at your parent as well as at
Heather. Still, it is quite possible that Heather did her best.
Certainly, Martha needs to learn to be more empathetic and
less critical of her teammate. So how could her parent better

handle this problem? How could her parent show understanding for Martha's frustrations and yet teach her a valuable lesson about teamwork?

Here is how it might have been handled:

MARTHA: That stupid Heather! She always messes up. We could have won our game today if she hadn't screwed up.

PARENT: The game didn't go well today. (What-You-Meant Statement)

MARTHA: No! Heather dropped the ball and the other team scored the winning run.

PARENT: You're angry that Heather dropped the ball. You think you could have won if she had caught it. Could it be that Heather tried her best and she, too, is disappointed? (Walk-In-Their-Shoes Statement)

MARTHA: But we lost because of her!

PARENT: You're really upset about losing today's game. Your team has won most of its other games. (Walk-In-Their-Shoes Statement)

MARTHA: This was a key game.

PARENT: It's great to win. Losing is disappointing. Working as a team is important if the team is to do well in the future. I remember times when you dropped the ball, and now you're leading the team in catching. I bet with your help Heather would get better too. With you coaching her, she could do better the next time, and the whole team would benefit. Would you help her? She sure could use your help. And I bet she'd be happy to have it. You're a good coach. Now, let's have our dinner.

With that, Martha was satisfied. She went on to help Heather become a better baseball player. As parents, we need to learn to hear our children and let them know we understand their feelings. This encourages them to listen to us. When they listen, we can often help them make more mature decisions. In the second dialogue, Martha knew she had been heard and that her feelings mattered. So she became willing to rethink her initial outburst and consider a constructive solution. By using a Walk-In-Their-Shoes Statement, Martha's parent encouraged her to try to understand her teammate's mistake. This let Martha decide to help Heather rather than criticize her.

Listening to the child is the most important part of making a good Walk-In-Their-Shoes Statement. When children know you respect them and care enough about how they feel to *really listen* to them, they feel encouraged and self-confident. They are then willing to be more cooperative and open to suggestions. How did *you* feel the last time someone truly listened to you? We all want others to know how we feel, and we appreciate it when they listen to us carefully and sincerely. The Walk-In-Their-Shoes Statement lets children know that they are heard, understood, respected, and cared for.

In fact, you can improve all your relationships by using this communication skill. You have the most to gain by using it with the people closest to you. Since your children, your spouse, and even your close friends are the very people most likely to be hurt by criticism or advice, the Walk-In-Their-Shoes Statement is especially useful. Be sure to pay careful attention and to practice both steps consistently. If you recognize their feelings and refocus their attention on a past or future success, you will reap the benefits of more open and positive communication.

8

"You Believe That . . ."

Support-Their-Thinking Statement (STT)

*Y*ou have seen how the Walk-In-Their-Shoes Statement considers your child's feelings. This next skill focuses on your child's *thinking*. The Support-Their-Thinking Statement (STT) is useful whenever you want to reply to what your children believe rather than what they feel. With the Walk-In-Their-Shoes Statement, you accept your children's *feelings* as okay. With the Support-Their-Thinking Statement, you accept their *opinions* and *beliefs* as being sound and reasonable *to them*.

Support-Their-Thinking Statement

Step 1. Children value their opinions. Let your words and actions say, "I know you have your own reasons for believing as you do. I respect your point of view."

Step 2. Support them totally if you agree with them. Give them additional information to help them to think more clearly if you disagree.

All parenting styles use Support-Their-Thinking Statements.

Here's How

1. "That's a fine idea." *(total support)*
2. "You could wait until this afternoon to get the tickets. Going to the ticket office early would get us the best choice of seats." *(give additional information)*
3. "Staying up for the late show sounds like fun. Remember last time you stayed up so late? You were too tired in the morning; you missed the fair." *(give additional information)*

Statements your child makes with which you agree are rarely a problem for you. In such a case, you might say, "Yes, I agree with you completely," or more simply, "You're right." In either case, you support your child's point of view.

For instance, your daughter might say to you, "It isn't fair that girls can't play on boys' hockey teams." If you support that opinion, you might use a Support-Their-Thinking Statement like the following:

PARENT: No doubt about it. Young women should be
          able to play on school hockey teams.

Sometimes children may not carefully think through an
issue. Then a parent can use the Support-Their-Thinking
Statement to give them *additional information.*

If, for example, you had reservations about the above
opinion about girls on boys' hockey teams, you might make
a Support-Their-Thinking Statement like:

PARENT: Many people agree with you. School officials
          would have to approve.

You supported your child's viewpoint, then added what
else he or she needed to know. Here is other additional
information the parent might have given:

PARENT: I see your point. Many school officials feel
          that heavy contact sports may present special
          problems for young women.

Even when you add information, you must still accept
your child's opinion. You do not have to agree with the facts.
Acceptance is not the same thing as agreement. When you
disagree, simply offer additional facts for your children to
consider. When they know the real facts, they will often
change their opinions.

Of course, sometimes children will not change their
minds, especially when they feel forced to defend what they
think. Using a Support-Their-Thinking Statement that gives
additional information at such a time says to your child, "I
hear what you're saying. Here are some more facts to consider." While you may disagree with your child, with the
Support-Their-Thinking Statement you recognize your child's

right to have an opinion. Doing so reduces, and may even end, conflict.

The portion of the Support-Their-Thinking Statement that adds new information also gives your child a new way to think, which may lead to a change of mind. On the other hand, statements such as "You're just a child. What do you know?" or "You're wrong! Marijuana is harmful. No one should smoke it" only boxes children into corners which they feel they must defend. Support-Their-Thinking Statements tell children you hear them and respect their opinions. When children feel their parents respect them and their ideas, they are more willing to listen to their parents' views.

You can see, then, that the Support-Their-Thinking Statement is also a two-step skill. First, accept that the opinion is valid — at least in your child's mind. Second, give your total support if you agree or introduce additional information if you disagree.

Practice 1

Of the following expressions, check those that are the first step of the Support-Their-Thinking Statement: accepting the child's point of view:

_____	That's a good point.
_____	You've got a good idea there.
_____	You shouldn't feel that way.
_____	I completely disagree with you.
_____	You might be right.

Answers:
That's a good point. You've got a good idea there.
You might be right.

In this next Support-Their-Thinking Statement, underline the part that accepts the child's opinion and put brackets [] at the beginning and end of the part that adds information:

TEEN: I shouldn't have to do jobs for my allowance.
PARENT: Many teenagers think as you do. You're learning to be an adult. Adults have to earn their money. Earning your allowance is an important step in learning to be an adult.

Answers:
Many teenagers think as you do.

[You're learning to be an adult. Adults have to earn their money. Earning your allowance is an important step in learning to be an adult.]

Notice that in the above situation the parent does not agree with the teenager. Yet the parent first accepts the teen's opinion and only then introduces more information. The additional facts not only recognize the teen's ideas about having an allowance, but also indicate why working for it is necessary. This approach says, "I hear what you are saying. Here is something more to consider."

Practice 2

In each of the following examples, a child expresses an opinion. Three Support-Their-Thinking Statements then follow. After each, indicate whether the parent gives total support or adds additional information because he or she doesn't totally agree with the child.

TEEN: I think kids in high school are mature enough to see R-rated movies.

Statement 1: You may be right, if they are mature enough to set standards of good taste.

_____ total support
_____ additional information given

Statement 2: You're right. Teenagers will act responsibly if we treat them as mature individuals.

_____ total support
_____ additional information given

Statement 3: You have a point. Maturity also means you follow rules until they're changed.

_____ total support
_____ additional information given

Answers:
Statement 1: additional information given, Statement 2: total support, Statement 3: additional information given

TEEN: I think we should have just a pass/fail grading system at school.

Statement 1: I agree. The struggle for good grades can get in the way of real learning.

_____ total support
_____ additional information given

Statement 2: There are some problems with the present grading system. I guess we'd have to look at what's right and what's wrong with each system. That way we can find out which is better.

    _____   total support
    _____   additional information given

Statement 3: Many people agree with you. Most colleges and the community believe the letter-grade system is better.

    _____   total support
    _____   additional information given

Answers:
Statement 1: total support, Statement 2: additional information given, Statement 3: additional information given

THE CHALLENGE OF THIS SKILL

The Walk-In-Their-Shoes Statement accepts children's *feelings* as real while the Support-Their-Thinking Statement accepts their right to have *opinions*.

Like the Walk-In-Their-Shoes Statement, the Support-Their-Thinking Statement may be a challenge to master at first. This is especially true when you are trying to add information, which suggests that you don't completely agree and may force children to defend their points of view. Successfully using the Support-Their-Thinking Statement requires a certain mind set. Like hundreds of other parents, with practice you will learn to handle it easily.

First, recognize and accept that young people usually believe in their points of view. You must accept their views, remembering that acceptance does not mean agreement.

Second, if you want to change their minds, you are more likely to succeed if you give them enough facts. It's not what *you* think that will change their minds. It's what *they* think — after hearing what you think.

When you let children know you accept (not necessarily agree with) their points of view, you show them you believe in their ability to think and reason. When you add information, you help them form better opinions.

We all hold our points of view for our own good reasons. We all form opinions based on whatever information we have. Whether accurate or inaccurate, biased or unbiased, complete or partial, we all believe our opinions are reasonable.

CHECKUP

The Support-Their-Thinking Statement first accepts the child's opinion as _____, at least in the child's mind, and gives _____ or _____.

Possible Answers:
valid, total support, additional information

AVOID USING "BUT" AND "HOWEVER"

In the Support-Their-Thinking Statements you have looked at so far, notice that the parents all avoided using the words "but" and "however" when offering additional information. If I say, "That's a good point, but . . ." I'm really saying, "It's not such a good point. I take exception to it." When parents use words like "but" and "however," they often force children to defend what their parents want them to change. When you are adding additional information in the Support-Their-Thinking Statement, offer only what the child may need to understand without using "but" or "however," especially when you wish to encourage your children to change their points of view.

Practice 3

With this point in mind, spend time making Support-Their-Thinking Statements of your own. Since total support is easy to give, limit your Support-Their-Thinking Statements to those offering *additional information*. Try coming up with two different pieces of additional information you might give.

Consider the first example. Drew, aged 16, is the oldest of three children. Her family rents a three-bedroom house. The parents have one bedroom, Drew's 13-year-old brother Stewart has another, and Drew must share the third with her 11-year-old sister Pat.

> DREW: It's not fair. Stewart gets a bedroom all to himself, and I have to share mine with Pat. I need some privacy.

Additional Information 1:

_____

_____

Additional Information 2:

_____

_____

Possible Answers:

Additional Information 1: "You have a point, Drew. You are more responsible now. I know it's hard to share. If you'd like to sit, we can talk about this problem. There may be a way to get you more privacy."

Additional Information 2: "You do have less privacy than Stewart. Unfortunately, we only have three bedrooms."

Drew does have a point. Additional information should recognize her need for privacy, if not her right to it.

These are both satisfactory approaches. The first option is especially appropriate if the parent can find inexpensive ways to divide the girls' room and give them both more privacy. In a similar situation, the older girl was happy with the privacy a makeshift basement bedroom gave her. Thinking up creative solutions to seemingly unsolvable problems is a good way to avoid anger and frustration. If there are no creative solutions, giving additional information at least recognizes Drew's wish for privacy.

Practice 4

How would you respond to this child?

> CHILD: I know I've got good grades, but I don't see why everyone is pushing me to go to college. I'd rather go to work.

Additional Information 1:

_____

_____

Additional Information 2:

_____

_____

Possible Answers:

Additional Information 1: "You have a point. Perhaps if you
   worked for awhile before going to college, you would
   have a better idea of what college could do for you."

Additional Information 2: "I used to feel as you do. More
   and more, with so many people now looking for jobs,
   employers are hiring only people who apply that have
   a college education."

Before going on, compare how the parent in the next two examples used the Support-Their-Thinking Statement:

JANE: (*stomps into house angrily*) Dad let Sydney have the car. I wanted to use it. He gets the car all the time just because he's a boy.

MOTHER: He has a date with Vera.

JANE: I'm sick of him getting the car whenever he wants. I never get it.

MOTHER: You had it last weekend.

JANE: (*angrier*) So did Sydney. I hate him!

MOTHER: Don't get smart or you won't get the car at all. Besides, you don't hate him.

JANE: It's not fair. He's older, so he gets the car whenever he wants. You always let him have his way.

MOTHER: That's it! Go to your room. You can't have the car for a month. Maybe now you'll appreciate that you get it at all.

Jane stomps off angrily, slamming the door behind her.

Jane's mother didn't get very far, did she? She should have let Jane know that she understood what Jane believed. Had she done so, Jane would have been more willing to listen. The mother also stressed only the way she wanted things done and seemed to ignore the fact that Jane believed she was being treated unfairly. Let's see how this problem might have been handled better. By providing additional information, Jane's mother could have changed the outcome:

JANE: (*stomps into house angrily*) Dad let Sydney have the car. I wanted to use it. He gets the car all the time just because he's a boy.

MOTHER: Sydney does get the car quite often. His dates don't drive though. The boys you've been seeing usually drive you where you're going. (acknowledges opinion, gives additional information)

JANE: I never get the car. He gets it whenever he wants it.

MOTHER: Sydney asked for the car last weekend. If you talk to Dad today, you can reserve the car for next weekend. (additional information)

JANE: It's not fair. He's older, so you let him have his way.

MOTHER: He does get it more often. He's been driving longer. (acknowledges opinion, gives additional information)

JANE: Now I have to wait until next weekend.

MOTHER: The car will be yours if Dad is not using it. (additional information)

JANE: But I wanted it today.

MOTHER: You need to ask for the car ahead of time like Sydney did. Then you can get your turn. Talk with Dad now, before he leaves. I'm sure he'll let you use the car next weekend. Can I drive you somewhere today? I have time this afternoon. (gives additional information)

JANE: Thanks, Mom. I'll call Brendan and see if that's okay with him. Maybe he can get his folks' car.

By letting Jane know that she understood what Jane believed, and by offering important additional information,

Jane's mother successfully resolved the problem. Jane was content with the outcome even though she would have preferred to have the car sooner.

You will find the Support-Their-Thinking Statement useful in many situations with your children. With practice, using this skill will become automatic.

9

"That-a-Way!"

Catch-Them-Doing-It-Right Statement (CTDR)

*W*e all have qualities of which we are proud. Some of us take pride in our creativity, others in having business sense, intelligence, and so forth. The Catch-Them-Doing-It-Right Statement encourages those qualities in which children can take pride. If they feel good about themselves, they will be more likely to succeed in what they do.

Catch-Them-Doing-It-Right Statement

Step 1.   Show approval.
Step 2.   Connect the approval to a
             quality the *child* values.
             The two steps may be:
             • Given separately.
             • Combined into one statement.
This is primarily an "Our Way"
parenting approach. It is also useful
with a "Your Way" style.

Here's How

1. "I'm pleased with your tidy room, Antonio. You've been very grown up."
   (two steps given separately, child values being grown up)
2. "That was a brave thing you did, standing up for your friend."
   (combined steps, child values being courageous)

The Catch-Them-Doing-It-Right Statement has two steps. First, you express your approval. Then you connect your approval to a quality your *child* values. You can do these steps separately or you can combine them. Here's an example of a Catch-Them-Doing-It-Right Statement given in two steps:

PARENT: I'm pleased with the way you took this phone message. You've been very responsible.

Here's one that combines the two steps of the skill into one statement:

PARENT: I like the thorough job you did.

Combined in this way, the two steps of the Catch-Them-Doing-It-Right Statement 1) show approval and 2) personalize the approval to a quality the *child* values. The first child valued being responsible and the second child valued being thorough.

Sometimes your Catch-Them-Doing-It-Right Statement will *imply* (rather than state) either of the steps. For example:

PARENT: That was a very grown-up job you did.

It is important that your approval be directed to a quality that your child really values. If you're unsure of exactly why your child might take pride in a particular act, you may omit Step 2 and only express your approval. Let your child decide what the approval means. Here is a lighthearted example of approval that might be at odds with values that Arnold Schwarzenegger holds dear:

PARENT: Arnold, the shine on your kitchen floor
                shows you're a meticulous housekeeper.

Assuming that we know something about Arnold, this approval really misses the mark! Sometimes it is better to leave out the reference to a specific value and use only a general statement of approval.

Practice 1

Below are some Catch-Them-Doing-It-Right Statements in which the parent implies the second step. After each, suggest what qualities the parent's approval might encourage in the child. Keep in mind that answers can vary widely.

PARENT: You've been a great help to me today.

_____

Possible Answers:
helpfulness, caring, cooperation

PARENT: I like the way you got the girls together.

_____

Possible Answers:
organization, leadership, being a team player

>   PARENT: I appreciate all the good work you did.

_____

Possible Answers:
being industrious, helpfulness, dependability, persistence

Practice 2
Show whether the following Catch-Them-Doing-It-Right Statements use both steps separately or both steps combined.

>   PARENT: I'm very pleased that you've all been
>   so cooperative.

>   _____   Both steps separately
>   _____   Both steps combined

Answer:
Both steps combined

>   PARENT: This is an excellent painting, Pablo. You're
>   very imaginative.

>   _____   Both steps separately
>   _____   Both steps combined

Answer:
Both steps separately

The Catch-Them-Doing-It-Right Statement uses your child's natural tendency to feel good when getting approval.

Even as adults, when someone approves of us we feel good about ourselves and feel inspired to do better. So do children.

GIVE APPROPRIATE APPROVAL

Approval must be both sincere and believable to the person receiving it. Approving of our children too enthusiastically for something they know is only average undermines their self-confidence and their trust in you.

For reasons of their own, some children find it difficult to accept any sort of approval, especially as they get older. It is important to handle such young people with care. For them, using only the first step of the Catch-Them-Doing-It-Right Statement is often the best approach.

In short, show approval of your children's behavior only when you know the approval will be acceptable and encouraging to them.

Practice 3

Take a few minutes to practice the Catch-Them-Doing-It-Right Statement. After each of the following situations, write two examples of your own. Use 1) both steps separately and 2) both steps combined.

The first situation concerns a child who puts a great deal of effort into things that he does. Unfortunately, at times he does so awkwardly. You have just checked to see how well he dressed himself for school, and found he had not completely tucked in his shirt.

Both Steps Separately:

_____

_____

Both Steps Combined:

_____

_____

Possible Answers:
Both Steps Separately: "You're getting very good at dressing
  yourself. I can see how hard you have been trying to get
  ready on your own."
Both Steps Combined: "I'm very pleased with the effort
  you've made to get yourself dressed."

You would encourage the child most if you ignored the
fact that he had not tucked his shirt in completely. If you
could not ignore it, you might ask, "May I tuck the rest of
your shirt in?"

The next child has written an imaginative story that
contains several grammar and spelling errors.

Both Steps Separately:

_____

_____

Both Steps Combined:

_____

_____

Possible Answers:
Both Steps Separately: "This is a well-thought-out story.
   You've shown a lot of imagination."
Both Steps Combined: "I like the imagination you showed
   in your story."

Finally, write Catch-Them-Doing-It-Right Statements for a child who plays a musical instrument, often without much enthusiasm. Today the child has made some progress.

Both Steps Separately:

_____

_____

Both Steps Combined:

_____

_____

Possible Answers:
Both Steps Separately: "That sounded good. I can see
   you've been working hard on your music."
Both Steps Combined: "I like the hard work you put into
   your music today."

FOCUS ON THE POSITIVE

It is important when giving approval to focus on the positive parts of a child's behavior. Even when a child's behavior is negative, there may be parts of it that demonstrate positive qualities that you want to encourage. By using a Catch-Them-

Doing-It-Right Statement, you can help a child see his or her positive attributes.

For example, a child who gets into a fistfight to defend a friend is demonstrating loyalty. You don't want your child fighting, yet being loyal to one's friends is an admirable trait — one to encourage. When you focus on the positive elements of children's behavior, you help children to do the same. In this way your children gain a sense of pride in what you *do* approve. You may follow your Catch-Them-Doing-It-Right Statement with an idea that will encourage them to use their skills for a positive purpose. Here is how it might sound:

> PARENT: You know we don't approve of fighting, Geri. Defending your friend shows that you are loyal, and loyalty to friends is important. Let's talk about other things you could have done to defend him and show your loyalty.

In this way, Catch-Them-Doing-It-Right Statements can be used to change behavior by *downplaying negative* and *emphasizing positive* personal traits.

CHECKUP

The Catch-Them-Doing-It-Right Statement deals most closely with children's feelings about themselves. It encourages those qualities a child values and enhances the child's _____. The Catch-Them-Doing-It-Right Statement is a two-step skill. The first step is to _____ and the second step is to _____ _____. You may use both Catch-Them-Doing-It-Right Statement steps _____ or _____.

Possible Answers:
self-worth, show approval, connect the approval to a quality the child values, together, separately

THEY DID IT, SO CAN YOU!

When children are in trouble, they are least likely to listen to their parents. In such circumstances, children expect parents to be angry, so they usually become defensive. The communication skills in this section will help you to overcome your children's natural resistance to parental authority.

Now let's see how the eight communication skills you've learned so far have worked for other parents. Here is one parent's story:

Jon arrived home late from school one day. The principal had called earlier to say that Jon skipped his first class and went to the local donut shop with two other students. Jon's mother was not pleased. She did not approve of Jon's skipping class. The principal had already dealt with him by giving a week's detention. She did not want to punish him twice. Her problem was how to let him know how disappointed she was and yet show she supported him.

"Welcome home," she began. (Look-On-The-Bright-Side Statement)

Jon, who already knew about the call home, looked sheepishly at his mother and replied, "I'm sorry, Mom. I know I shouldn't have skipped first period, but Ed and Sean wanted me to go with them."

"If your friends skip, then you have to skip too." (Think-It-Over Statement) Clearly, this was not so.

"They'd have been on my case if I hadn't gone with them."

"You felt pressured to go," she confirmed. (What-You-Meant Statement)

"Wouldn't you, too, if your friends wanted you to do something?"

"Sometimes pressure from our friends can be more than we can handle," Mother said. (Walk-In-Their-Shoes Statement) "Usually your friends follow *you*."

"I didn't want to deal with it."

"You wanted to be a good friend, so you had to break the rules." (What-You-Meant Statement)

"I know I should have gone to school, but I really wanted to be with them too." In his mind, Jon's dilemma was real.

Though his mother could not agree with his decision, she could understand it. "I'm glad you wanted to be a good friend. I'm also very encouraged that you recognize you shouldn't have skipped class. (Catch-Them-Doing-It-Right Statement) What will you do next time?" (Tell-Me-What's-On-Your-Mind Question)

"Go to class. But it won't be easy. The guys won't like it."

"You've made the right decision. (Support-Their-Thinking Statement — total support) I believe you mean it. (Look-On-The-Bright-Side Statement) Maybe the boys will understand if you say no the next time. You might even set the example for them to follow. (Catch-Them-Doing-It-Right Statement) What do you want for dinner?"

This parent let her son know she understood his problem. She also gave positive support for what he would say to them the next time his friends invited him to skip class. What is more, because she spoke positively to Jon, he did not have to defend himself. He recognized his mistake and decided not to repeat it. She suggested Jon might be a good example for his friends the next time. By doing so, she also gave Jon a reason to act responsibly if they asked him to break school rules again.

In the next chapter, we have provided some additional Practice and Review Activities. They will give you further practice in using all the communication skills you have learned. The emphasis, though, is on the communication skills used for overcoming objections. If you feel confident that you have mastered the four skills in this section, please skip Chapter 10, and go on to Part 4 and learn the Skills for Solving Problems and Making Decisions With Your Child on page 185.

10

See What You've Learned!

*Y*ou have experienced how the various communication skills address different problems. For problems arising from your child's *feelings*, use a Walk-In-Their-Shoes Statement. If the problem relates to your child's *ideas* or *beliefs*, you might use a Support-Their-Thinking Statement. When your child's *pride* is at stake, the Catch-Them-Doing-It-Right Statement is most effective. Remember, too, to *think positively*! Whatever skill you employ, use Look-On-The-Bright-Side Statements.

This chapter gives you an opportunity to practice all the communication skills you have learned. To focus your practice, we have emphasized the more challenging Skills for Overcoming Your Child's Objections rather than the first four Skills for Discovering What's On Your Child's Mind. Be alert to opportunities to use skills from both sections, concentrating on the Skills for Overcoming Your Child's Objections whenever possible. Strengthen and practice the skills you've just learned.

In the following pages you will find three situations for practice. Carefully read the parent's remarks in the first situation, and identify the specific skills she uses in the space provided after each of her statements. The next two situations offer you the chance to consider what skills you yourself might find most appropriate. Use your own judgment and keep in mind that many correct responses are possible. After you respond, look at the answers. We have included examples of several equally effective ways to handle each problem.

JAYDON and ZNOBIA'S ZOO TRIP

Background Information
Parent: Mrs. Patel
Children: Jaydon (10) and Znobia (8)

A few minutes ago Mrs. Patel packed the car to go to the zoo for a picnic with her children. A phone call delayed them. Now both children are restless and impatient. As they are about to get into the car, Mrs. Patel sees Jaydon give Znobia a push.

Mrs. Patel does not know what the pushing is all about. She suspects the children are arguing about who will sit in the front beside her. She handles the trouble quickly. After each of Mrs. Patel's remarks, name the communication skill. (Notice that all are phrased positively.)

MRS. PATEL: I understand you both want to sit in the front. You are safer in the back. Jaydon, you sit on this side. Znobia, you buckle up over there.

Answer:
Support-Their-Thinking Statement (one which gives additional information)

Mrs. Patel could have handled this another way. She could have placed herself close to Jaydon and Znobia while speaking to them. Moving closer would make the children more aware of her physical presence and focus them more on her and less on each other. She could also physically move either child if need be, and they know it. I am not suggesting this maneuver be used to threaten children with physical punishment. Rather, Mrs. Patel's moving toward the children is conveying, "I mean business." This tactic would be enhanced if Mrs. Patel were also to say something like, "Would you like to cooperate, or would one or both of you like to go back into the house and stay behind?" Then the children will have even fewer options and be even less likely to continue their quarreling. If they do continue, Mrs. Patel simply has to do what she said she would do. It will not be long before the children get the message: you can go to the zoo only when you behave appropriately.

> MRS. PATEL: Jaydon, thank you for loading the trunk of the car. It shows you can get things done. Buckle up on this side.

> MRS. PATEL: Znobia, thank you for remembering the blanket. Sit over there.

Answers:
Catch-Them-Doing-It-Right Statement (both steps
   separately), Catch-Them-Doing-It-Right Statement
   (second step implied)

Here is a third way she might have handled the situation:

> MRS. PATEL: Jaydon, what's wrong?

> JAYDON: She pushed me first.

MRS. PATEL: Znobia?

ZNOBIA: It was an accident!
MRS. PATEL: I see. You didn't mean to bump him.

Answers:
Tell-Me-What's-On-Your-Mind Question, Tell-Me-What's-
On-Your-Mind Question (implying, "What have you to
say about it, Znobia?"), What-You-Meant Statement

Finally, she might try yet another approach:

MRS. PATEL: I know you are both anxious to go on a
picnic. We'll have to help each other if
we're to get there and have fun.

Answer:
Walk-In-Their-Shoes Statement (alternative direction)

Since Mrs. Patel saw all that happened, she looks sharply
at both of them. Jaydon feels the need to speak:

JAYDON: She pushed me first.
ZNOBIA: I did not. I tripped.
MRS. PATEL: Yes, I saw what happened. Both of you
were rushing to sit in the front.

JAYDON:	She pushed me.
MRS. PATEL:	I know you thought she did. You pushed back before you knew she had tripped accidentally.

Answers:

Both of the above are Support-Their-Thinking Statements (ones which give additional information)

Mrs. Patel might have handled this simple situation in many other ways. These are only a few of the ways you could use each of the communication skills you've learned in this section. Now let's move on to another example.

Background Information

Parent: Mr. Situ

Daughter: Kim (15)

Kim has always been a good student. To her surprise, she has just failed a math test. Dismayed, she asks her father, Mr. Situ, for help. Kim did very poorly on the problem-solving section of the test, though earlier she had handled problem solving easily. Mr. Situ believes that Kim would have gotten the right answers if she had simply checked her arithmetic more thoroughly.

In this practice, write an example of the required communication skill Mr. Situ will use in response to Kim. Several answers are possible in each case. Mr. Situ has just returned from work. Kim is going to show him her math quiz paper. She has her math paper in hand, and is looking extremely unhappy.

THE MATH PAPER

KIM: Dad?

MR. SITU: Yes, Kim, what is it?

KIM: Look at my math paper. I can't under-
          stand it. I thought I knew the work, but
          I got hardly any answers right. I
          studied, but I still failed.

Deal first with Kim's obvious feelings of distress by using
a Walk-In-Their-Shoes Statement.

_____

_____

Possible Answers:
"I know how hard you've studied. Let's see if we can tell what happened."
"I can see why you're upset. You've done so well in the past. This weekly quiz will not affect your final semester grade, Kim."
"You feel very disappointed about the grade. You worked hard and you still failed. What can we do to keep this from happening again?"

Mr. Situ's Walk-In-Their-Shoes Statement leads Kim in another direction:

MR. SITU: It's upsetting to fail a test after you've studied so hard. Let's see if we can find out what happened.

KIM: I don't know what happened. I did all the math problems just the way the teacher taught us, but I got the answers wrong anyway.

Kim seems to understand the math concepts, but didn't check her arithmetic. Phrase a Catch-Them-Doing-It-Right Statement to bolster Kim's self-esteem.

_____

_____

Possible Answers:
"I like the way you solved the problems. It shows you understand the ideas."
"Your problem solving shows you understand the ideas."

"You understand the problem-solving ideas. Your math is giving you trouble."

"I like the way you solved the problems."

Let's see how Mr. Situ handled the situation:

MR. SITU: You went about solving the problems the right way. It's clear you have paid attention in class and understand the ideas.

KIM: But I got the wrong answers.

Use a Support-Their-Thinking Statement to reply to Kim's remark that she got the wrong answers.

_____

_____

Possible Answers:

"You did get many right, Kim. You had trouble with the math calculations."

"True, your answers were sometimes incorrect. Your problem-solving methods were right."

Perhaps you responded as Mr. Situ did:

MR. SITU: You got many answers right, Kim. You'd have had all of them right if you'd been accurate in your calculations.

KIM: I messed up the arithmetic, huh?

Now phrase a Catch-Them-Doing-It-Right Statement that would help Kim to think for *herself* about how those errors occurred.

_____

_____

Possible Answers:
"That's right. You see where the problem is."
"Now you're thinking."

Mr. Situ combines a Catch-Them-Doing-It-Right Statement and a Support-Their-Thinking Statement adding additional information. He first accepts her assessment of the problem, then points out that her first error made the final answer wrong.

MR. SITU: You have it now, Kim. Good for you.
              You're right. The problem is in the
              earlier arithmetic.
KIM: Yeah, I guess I didn't see the first
              mistake and that made all the rest of my
              work wrong.

Mr. Situ lets Kim know that if she had checked carefully, she wouldn't have gotten the problems wrong in the first place.

A Support-Their-Thinking Statement giving additional information might be effective here.

_____

_____

Possible Answers:

"That's right. You'd have caught the first mistake if you'd checked your work."

"Yes. You must check your work to avoid getting the problems wrong."

Your Support-Their-Thinking Statement might have been similar to Mr. Situ's:

MR. SITU: It's important to catch that first mistake. You'd have found it if you had checked your work carefully.

KIM: I know . . . but I wanted to get all the problems done. This test was important.

Now phrase a Think-It-Over Statement that would point out what's wrong with Kim's idea that working quickly is more important than getting it right.

_____

_____

Possible Answers:

"Finishing the test quickly was better than getting the answers right."

"You'd rather finish the test than get the answers right."

Like Mr. Situ, you might have used the following Think-It-Over Statement pointing to the trouble with Kim's thinking:

MR. SITU: Rushing through the problems and getting them wrong was more important

	than checking them to make sure they were right.
KIM:	Yeah, I see what you mean.

Finish this conversation with a What-You-Meant Statement of Kim's unspoken intention to check her work from now on.

_____

_____

Possible Answers:
"Then you'll be sure to check carefully in the future."
"Now that you know how important checking is, you'll check your work from now on."

Here is what Mr. Situ says:

MR. SITU:	From now on you'll check your work before handing it in.

Background Information
Parent: Mrs. Wright
Son: Joe (17)

It's a school holiday. Joe has been home with some friends while Mrs. Wright was shopping. On returning home, Mrs. Wright smells the unmistakable odor of cigarettes. What is more, many community groups have been asking the police to enforce the cigarette laws relating to minors.

Joe is a good person who gets along well with his mother. Often he has a good relationship with his father, too, though they run into trouble when Mr. Wright's expectations are too

SOMETHING'S UP——⟶

high. Lately Joe has gotten into several minor scrapes, and twice in the past year Mr. Wright has been called to go down to the police station.

In the following practice you will choose what communication skills you would use to respond to Joe's statements. You will then phrase a response that follows the steps of the skill. Think carefully and take your time before choosing the skills and phrasing your responses. Would you expect Joe to offer both intellectual and emotional objections to your statements? He knows that smoking is against the law for minors, but he will surely defend his actions. He will also be upset that his mother caught him, especially in front of his friends. This will make him even more defensive. If you think he will use both intellectual and emotional objections, remember to use Think-It-Over Statements and Support-Their-Ideas Statements. Because Joe has a good relationship with his mother, you might also consider using Catch-Them-Doing-It-Right Statements.

The scene begins as Mrs. Wright enters the house, sees smoke, and smells cigarettes. Obviously, Joe has not been smoking alone. Mrs. Wright is reluctant to confront him, but realizes that she must. Consider what objections Joe might raise as you decide what communication skills you will use to begin the conversation:

Communication Skill:

_____

Your opening remark:

_____

Possible Answers:
Tell-Me-What's-On-Your-Mind Question: "What's going on here, Joe?" (question that makes a statement)

Mrs. Wright might have chosen one or two Give-Me-Specific-Information Questions, but note how using them in the response that follows is not a good idea:

MRS. WRIGHT: Don't you know that smoking cigarettes is not legal at your age? Aren't you concerned about what would have happened if the police had caught you or showed up at the house? You know they have been cracking down on kids your age caught smoking.

Instead, Mrs. Wright might have begun with a What-You-Meant Statement:

MRS. WRIGHT: Joe, you know that smoking cigarettes is against the law at your age. I'll have to let your father know about this too.

Why did she begin with this What-You-Meant Statement instead of with a Give-Me-Specific-Information Question?

_____

Answer:
The What-You-Meant Statement will avoid a showdown, while a Give-Me-Specific-Information Question would only encourage Joe to defend himself: "Everyone does it. Besides, how could the police have found out?"

Instead, Joe responds:

JOE: Aw, c'mon, Mom. It won't happen again.

What might your response be?

_____

_____

Possible Answers:
Tell-Me-What's-On-Your-Mind Question: "How can I be sure of that?"
Give-Me-Specific-Information Question: "Joe, can I count on that?"

What-You-Meant Statement (of intent): "I have your word, then, Joe."

Walk-In-Their-Shoes Statement: "I know you're in a jam and I'm sorry. I have to tell your father."

Support-Their-Thinking Statement (with additional information): "I'm sure you didn't consider how serious this is, Joe. Let's see what we can do to make sure it doesn't happen again."

Mrs. Wright decides to use a Catch-Them-Doing-It-Right Statement with Joe:

MRS. WRIGHT: That's a worthy promise, Joe.

Or she uses a Think-It-Over Statement:

MRS. WRIGHT: You feel I shouldn't act like a parent.
JOE: Aw, Mom, please. I don't want to be grounded. I promise I won't do it again. I'm going to stay out of trouble from now on.

What would you say next?

_____

_____

Possible Answers:

Tell-Me-What's-On-Your-Mind Question: "How are you going to stay out of trouble?"

Give-Me-Specific-Information Question: "Are you going to stop smoking?"

What-You-Meant Statement: "You're afraid of what will happen when your father finds out."

Think-It-Over Statement: "You're sure your promises will keep you out of trouble now."

Walk-In-Their-Shoes Statement: "I know you're upset, Joe. I'm sure this is the last time this will happen."

Support-Their-Thinking Statement: "I sympathize with what you're saying. I must deal with this problem, and your father has a right to know."

As she moves to the living room with Joe, Mrs. Wright replies with a Catch-Them-Doing-It-Right Statement:

MRS. WRIGHT: That's a wise decision, Joe.

JOE: Mom, after you guys talk about it, you'll ground me.

Write your response to Joe.

_____

_____

Possible Answers:

Tell-Me-What's-On-Your-Mind Question: "What could we do instead?"

Give-Me-Specific-Information Question: "Why would we do that?"

What-You-Meant Statement: "You don't want us to ground you."

Think-It-Over Statement: "You believe there's no reason to tell your dad."

Support-Their-Thinking Statement: "You're right. Your dad will ground you and so will I."

Mrs. Wright continues the discussion with a Walk-In-Their-Shoes Statement:

MRS. WRIGHT: Joe, I know it's tough to be in a jam like this. When you tell your dad that it won't happen again, make sure you keep your word.

As they continue, Joe blurts out:

JOE: It's a stupid law, anyway!

What would you say now?

_____

_____

Possible Answers:
Tell-Me-What's-On-Your-Mind Question: "What do you think would be a better way to deal with cigarette smoking?"
Give-Me-Specific-Information Question: "Do you think there shouldn't be any rules about minors smoking?"
What-You-Meant Statement: "You think it's unfair."
Think-It-Over Statement: "Cigarettes are good for your health."
Walk-In-Their-Shoes Statement: "You feel angry that there is a law against minors smoking."

Mrs. Wright uses a Support-Their-Thinking Statement:

MRS. WRIGHT: Perhaps. Many parents and community groups, even young people, want to promote health among young people.

We leave Joe and Mrs. Wright now as they continue their talk about whether or not the smoking laws are fair.

BRIDGE BUILDING

Our goal in each of the above problems was to increase your problem-handling skills. During the next week, you will talk with many people: your children, your spouse, other parents, and coworkers. You will also hear other people talking.

Listen carefully to yourself and to others. Listen for a chance to use Look-On-The-Bright-Side Statements, Walk-In-Their-Shoes Statements, Support-Their-Thinking Statements, and Catch-Them-Doing-It-Right Statements.

In a notebook used just for this purpose, write down the disagreements you hear. Note what the people involved say. Record the communication skills you might have used to avoid or remedy these disagreements. Try to find one or two incidents for each of the next seven days.

An example of your entries might be:

SITUATION: I heard a parent giving directions to his young child.

PARENT SAID: If you don't pick up your toys, you can't go to the playground.

SUBSTITUTE: You may go to the playground when you have picked up your toys. (Look-On-The-Bright-Side Statement)

Also write down any Support-Their-Thinking Statements and Think-It-Over Statements you might have used. You could also check newspaper or magazine stories for examples of negative phrasing and change the wording to Look-On-The-Bright-Side Statements.

MORE BRIDGE BUILDING

Being positive in negative situations is challenging. Overcoming children's resistances can be even more so. When children know you believe in and understand them, they stop being defensive. When you find the "up" in the "down" side of your children's actions, they will often let you guide them. They feel closer to you when they believe you care about what they think and how they feel.

You *learn* to have a positive attitude. You are not born with one. You also learn to see someone else's point of view. The more you practice, the more these skills will become a part of you.

If you want additional practice with Catch-Them-Doing-It-Right and Support-Their-Thinking Statements, try this activity: Look for some good in the activity, even when your child does something wrong. For example, talking back may show courage or a willingness to stand up for what one believes. Getting into mischief may show the child has spunk and can plan well.

Of course, you must object when a child does something wrong. Depending on your judgment, the behavior may call for a reprimand or punishment. Even so, the good parts of the bad behavior may provide the key to shift the child's future actions in the right direction. If your child gets into trouble this coming week, include Catch-Them-Doing-It-Right Statements and Support-Their-Thinking Statements such as these:

Catch-Them-Doing-It-Right Statement: "You know, it took courage to do that."

Support-Their-Thinking Statement: "I understand you dislike having a curfew. If you are willing to sit with me and talk calmly about it, we can see if we can do something about it."

Handling situations this way will show how trustworthy your child can be when you appeal to his or her sense of pride and responsibility. After doing some of these activities, reread Part 3: "I Don't Want To!" — Overcoming Your Child's Objections. Then, if you want to see how you are doing, ask your children to tell you how *they* feel about what you have done. This will help you make these communication skills natural and automatic. Your children, too, will benefit from talking about this. Go for it!

THEY DID IT, SO CAN YOU!

A positive attitude goes a long way to help deal with difficulties. It's a matter of "looking at the cup as half full, not half empty." With these communication skills, we can create good results from bad situations. Giving approval, if only for the good intentions of sometimes "bad" behavior, shows children we are on their side. They begin to feel we understand.

Here's how my wife and I used positively phrased communication skills to break down some barriers in our family interactions:

"Hello. What's the matter? You're where? Meet me at the entrance and I'll pick you up there." Jason hung up the phone and removed the car keys from the hook. "I'll be back in awhile!" he shouted from the kitchen. "I have to go out."

We didn't know he was going to the drive-in movie on the other side of town to pick up Deidre, our daughter. She had called to say she needed him right away.

The first hour passed, then the second. We grew more nervous with each tick of the clock. Three hours passed before the kids arrived home. Deidre had obviously been crying.

"Where have you been?" (Give-Me-Specific-Information Question) I asked anxiously. "You said you were going to the show. What happened to you? (Tell-Me-What's-On-Your-Mind Question) I thought you were out with Renzo."

That was the wrong thing to do. Deidre began to cry again as Jason jumped in:

"Just wait! Listen to what happened to her. Tell him, Deidre."

"I'm sorry, Deidre," I said. "You're very upset. I should have let you explain before pouncing on you. (Walk-In-Their-Shoes Statement) Sit down and tell us about it."

"It's not Jason's fault," Deidre said. "I called him to come and get me. He was only trying to help. When he got me, I was so upset I didn't want to come home right away, so he took me to the coffee shop. That's where we've been."

"Thank you for helping, Jason." I said. (Catch-Them-Doing-It-Right Statement) "It's good to know Deidre can count on you when she needs to. (Catch-Them-Doing-It-Right Statement) What happened? (Tell-Me-What's-On-Your-Mind Question) Where's Renzo? (Give-Me-Specific-Information Question)

DEIDRE'S SITUATION

Was there an accident on the way to the movies?" (Give-Me-Specific-Information Question)

"No, nothing like that," Jason said. "Give her a minute. You can see she's upset."

"We were supposed to go to a movie," Deidre continued. "When we got over to the mall, Renzo saw two of his buddies and pulled the car over to talk to them. When they found out we were going to the show, they opened the back door of the car and said they'd go with us. Renzo thought that was a great idea. But they'd been drinking. They said, 'Let's go to the drive-in movie, we've got some booze.' I was scared!"

"You were afraid because they'd been drinking," (What-You-Meant Statement) Rotraud, my wife, responded calmly, encouraging Deidre to go on.

"Wouldn't you be? I didn't want to be at the drive-in with three guys, and two of them drunk. I didn't know what to do. Everything was happening so fast. We were already there before I could do anything. Nobody asked me and I was scared to say no. I didn't know what his friends would do."

Deidre worried about what we might think. "Things happened too fast for you to know what to do," (What-You-Meant Statement) I offered. "You're home safe now." (Look-On-The-Bright-Side Statement)

"How did you get hold of Jason?" (Give-Me-Specific-Information Question) Rotraud asked.

"When they parked the car, they all started drinking. I got really scared then. So I said I had to go to the restroom. They let me out of the car and I went to the snack bar. I phoned home right away and played video games until Jason came. I guess the guys were too busy drinking to look for me."

"We appreciate your helping her, Jason. You really got her out of a tough spot." (Catch-Them-Doing-It-Right Statement) We were all thankful Deidre was safe! "You're still pretty upset," I continued. (What-You-Meant Statement)

"I was really scared! I didn't want to go there. I didn't know what else to do."

"You did really well," I assured her. (Catch-Them-Doing-It-Right Statement) "You were fast on your feet, if you ask me. You got yourself out of what could have been a dangerous situation."(Catch-Them-Doing-It-Right Statement)

Deidre had done well. She was safe. Now Jason needed some encouragement:

"Jason, I'm proud of you. You're her knight in shining armor!" (Catch-Them-Doing-It-Right Statement)

"I couldn't leave her there when she needed me."

"I'm glad you came and got me. And . . . thanks for taking me to the coffee shop. I really needed to talk." Deidre was more relaxed now as she leaned over and hugged her brother. Rotraud and I joined in.

"What are you going to do now?" I asked. (Tell-Me-What's-On-Your-Mind Question)

"Well, that's the last time I'm going out with Renzo, that's for sure. I wonder if he knows I'm gone yet." For the first time since coming home, Deidre laughed.

"How about coffee? You must be as tired as I am." (Walk-In-Their-Shoes Statement)

Rotraud yawned. "I'm tired. I'd like to get to bed."

"I'm too hyped up to sleep," Jason chimed in as he headed to the kitchen.

"I want to stay up and talk with Jason awhile. You guys go ahead . . . and . . . thanks." Deidre hugged each of us good night.

"You both did well tonight. It's great to know you look after each other. (Catch-Them-Doing-It-Right State-ment) Good night, all." I yawned too.

Deidre had expected us to be angry because she went to the drive-in, but criticizing her or Jason would only have made them defensive. Instead, our support and understanding reassured and encouraged her. We showed the children that we felt they had handled the problem well, and our approach helped to calm Deidre down. By using the four Skills for Overcoming Your Child's Objections, we encouraged the children to do the right thing the next time, and we also strengthened their confidence in us as parents. As a result, both our children feel free to come to us with many of their problems. And if not to us, they go to each other. Now, years later and well into adulthood, they continue to watch out for one another.

PRACTICE ROLE-PLAYS

On page 283 you will find role-plays that allow you to practice the communication skills of this section. Practicing with other adults before you use the communication skills with your children is helpful to many people.

In the next section, you will learn skills that help you solve problems and make decisions with your children.

FINISHED!

Take a break before you go on to the next part. Think about what you have learned so far, and practice these communication skills before learning the next four. Look for ways to use the communication skills you have already mastered, and practice those you haven't. If you forget how to use a particular communication skill, review it before you begin Part 4: "What WILL We Do?" — Solving Problems and Making Decisions With Your Child.

Part 4

"What WILL We Do?"

▶ Solving
Problems
and Making
Decisions
With Your
Child

Have you ever wondered how you could . . .

- help your children to solve their own problems?

- get your children to cooperate with you more?

- help your children so that they make the right decisions?

- set limits for your children so they will stay within them?

- offer your children encouragement when they are down?

This section will show you how to help your children solve problems and make decisions.

INTRODUCTION

The four remaining effective parenting skills will show you how to help your children solve problems and make decisions. These communication skills also help you become skillful with the parenting style you wish to use.

11

"What Should We Do?"

Solve-The-Problem Question (STP)

$\mathcal{T}$he first Skill for Solving Problems and Making Decisions With Your Child is the Solve-The-Problem Question. This is another two-step process.

Solve-The-Problem Question

Step 1. State the problem.

Step 2. Ask for possible solutions allowing for:

a. a broad range of solutions — "Your Way"

b. a narrow range of solutions — "Our Way"

c. a very narrow range of solutions — "My Way"

Or offer choices:

a. equal choices — "Your Way"

---

b. limited choices —
"Our Way"
c. unequal choices (Hobson's
Choice) — "My Way"

Here's How

1. "I promised we would have Saturday
morning together. Where would you
like to go?" ("Your Way," broad range
of solutions)
2. "We are going to buy a used car and
can afford a '96 or '97 model. What
kind should we look for?" ("Our
Way," narrow range of solutions)
3. "You may watch one cartoon show on
TV this morning, as long as it has no
violence and only lasts for 30
minutes. Which one would you like
to watch?" ("My Way," very narrow
range of solutions)
4. "We can have treats now. Do you
want ice cream, candy, or pizza?"
("Your Way," equal choices)
5. "It's time to clean up. Would you like
to help wash or dry?" ("Our Way,"
limited choices)
6. "You may color on the paper or put
the crayons away." ("My Way,"
unequal choices, Hobson's Choice)

The first step is to *state the problem*. Often problems go unsolved because neither the parent nor the child knows what the problem really is. For instance, a child who spills soda on homework might be upset about having to do it over or about the teacher's complaint about messy work; or he or she might just feel clumsy — even stupid. In fact, the child might be unhappy about all of these possibilities. Maybe you can dry off the homework to make it presentable, but that may not keep the child from feeling stupid. Knowing what the real problem is will help both you and your child to handle it in a better way.

Practice 1

Consider the following Solve-The-Problem Questions:

> PARENT 1: Children, we have to decide where to go on vacation. Where would you like to go?
>
> PARENT 2: On our vacation trip we want to do some sailing. Where would you like to do it?
>
> PARENT 3: Children, we want to plan a trip that will help you with your history and geography course at school next year. We have from July 24 until August 14. Where would you like to go?

While all three of these Solve-The-Problem Questions deal differently with the problem of where to go on a family vacation, they are different in one other important way. Can you tell what that difference is?

Answer:
They differ in how they limit the children's possible range of solutions.

Practice 2

Look at the three questions in Practice 1. Parents 1, 2, and 3 each asked the question differently. Fill in the blanks below with a 1, 2, or 3 to match the way the parent asked the Solve-The-Problem Question.

    a. _____   The Solve-The-Problem Question is stated
       "My Way" (very narrow).
    b. _____   The Solve-The-Problem Question is stated
       "Our Way" (narrow).
    c. _____   The Solve-The-Problem Question is stated
       "Your Way" (broad).

Answers:
a. 3, b. 2, c. 1

The Solve-The-Problem Question *requesting solutions,* then, can be asked in one of three ways: broadly, narrowly, or very narrowly. The broader the parents' request, the more the *children* control the decisions. The narrower the request, the more the *parents* keep control.

The Solve-The-Problem Question may also *offer choices.* If you want to keep the most control, you will offer several choices that are all acceptable to you, regardless of whether your children like them. We call these "unequal" choices. All parents must sometimes keep the decision-making authority for themselves.

If you want to give your children greater freedom to decide because you think they are particularly grown up, you will ask them to choose from several possibilities. Offering choices gives decision-making authority to children. Unequal choices allow you to keep the decision-making authority in your hands. Which approach you take depends on the parenting style you want to use and how grown up your children are.

Practice 3

Consider the following situation:

> PARENT: Children, the pavers are coming in the morning to work on the driveway, so it's going to be hard to get to the street while they're working. What can we do to make sure we get out of the house safely?

In the spaces below, indicate the steps in the Solve-The-Problem Question this parent used. Place a check on the appropriate lines.

    _____   Ignore the problem.
    _____   State the problem.
    _____   Ask for possible solutions.
    _____   Offer choices.

Answers:
1. State the problem, 2. Ask for possible solutions

Here's another example:

> PARENT: We need to decide what we will do on our Saturday morning outing. We can go to the zoo or to the beach.

This Solve-The-Problem Question offers the children equally desirable choices: the zoo or the beach. The parent could also ask the children for *their* choices, which would let them have even more control over the decision:

> PARENT: We need to decide what we will do on our
> Saturday morning outing. What do you
> suggest we do?

Asking children for their suggestions assumes that at least one of their ideas will solve the problem and you will be able to abide by it. It also gives them the broadest range of possibilities. This is a "Your Way" parenting approach.

Practice 4
Think of a problem you might wish to handle in this way, then write a Solve-The-Problem Question that asks for possible solutions.

_____

_____

Possible Answers:
"Robin and John, we're having a surprise party for Craig next month. What shall we do?"
"We have agreed to earn money for a new television by holding a garage sale. What should we sell?"

Instead of giving the children many choices, you can limit the number. Your child may or may not like the choices equally well. Look at this example of a Solve-The-Problem Question that offers equal choices:

> PARENT: Jacob and Sarah, we've only got one carnival
> ticket left for each of you. Do you want to go
> on the merry-go-round or the Ferris wheel?

Offering equal choices is an "Our Way" parenting approach.

This next parent offers unequal possibilities to a child who doesn't want to take a nap:

PARENT: It's time for your nap. Do you want to get into bed yourself, or would you like me to tuck you in?

In this case, the child didn't want to go to bed at all, so he didn't like either choice. The child could only choose between something he didn't like very much and something he didn't like at all. Most children will prefer one of these choices over the other. With practice, parents soon learn to offer choices that are acceptable both to the children and to themselves. Offering unequal choices makes this a "My Way" approach.

Salespeople often use this method to close a sale. They offer customers choices that assume the sale is already made, not asking *if* you want to buy, but "Would you like to put that on your credit card or on our monthly installment plan?" The salesperson is, in fact, giving you a choice between "yes" and "yes." It often works!

Practice 5

In the following Solve-The-Problem Question, mark whether the parent is requesting possible solutions, offering equal choices, or offering unequal choices:

PARENT: We need to get the housework done. Would you rather make the beds or do the vacuuming?

_____   possible solutions
_____   equal
_____   unequal

Answer:
equal (if the child would find them equal), unequal (if the child would prefer one to the other)

Practice 6
Below are examples of Solve-The-Problem Questions. Under each, write whether step two a) asks the children for possible solutions, b) offers equal choices, or c) offers unequal choices.

> PARENT: We need to prepare for our picnic. Would you like to make some sandwiches or would you rather pack the basket?

> ____   possible solutions
> ____   equal
> ____   unequal

Answer:
equal choices (if the children see them as equal)

> PARENT: You keep forgetting to bring your speller home. What can you do to remember it?

> ____   possible solutions
> ____   equal
> ____   unequal

Answer:
possible solutions

> PARENT: Children, I have to leave now. Would you like to hurry or should I leave without you?

_____ possible solutions
_____ equal
_____ unequal

Answer:
unequal choices

Often your children will not realize the options are unequal. By giving them a choice, you lower the chances for conflict. When you use this parenting approach, you are giving your child what we call a *Hobson's Choice*. (See insert on page 208 for an explanation about the term Hobson's Choice.) There is no *real* choice. This approach is particularly useful in situations like this one:

> PARENT: You've come home late the last two days. Will you try to get home on time, or would you prefer to have me come to school and walk you home in front of your friends?

Any Solve-The-Problem Question that offers specific choices limits your child to only those choices *you* offer. The Hobson's Choice restricts the possibilities even further by making your child choose the best of the *only two* choices *you* offer.

Practice 7

Let's take some time now to practice all forms of the Solve-The-Problem Question. First read the examples below, then write a Solve-The-Problem Question for each one.

In the first example, pretend you are a parent planning to help your two children plant their first vegetable garden. You want them to grow what they like to eat, so you will give them a lot of freedom to choose the vegetables they want.

Write a Solve-The-Problem Question that allows them to select the options:

_____

_____

Possible Answer:
"Today is a good day to plant your garden. What will you
   plant that you like to eat?"

Now pretend that one of your children is playing the radio so loudly it's upsetting the rest of the family. Phrase a Solve-The-Problem Question that offers a Hobson's Choice:

_____

_____

Possible Answer:
"Your radio is bothering the rest of us. Will you turn it
   down, or do you want me to do it for you?"

The choice is not "Will you turn your radio down or not?" The choice is *who* will turn it down and by *how much*.

In the following example, you want your children to help plan the upcoming family vacation. Phrase a Solve-The-Problem Question that gives them one of two options that are equal choices:

_____

_____

Possible Answer:
"We have to decide how we're going to spend our vacation.
Would you like to go to Vermont, or would you rather
spend the time in Virginia?"

The Solve-The-Problem Question that *asks for solutions*
lets children decide from any range of possibilities and is
limited only by how narrowly you ask the question. The Solve-
The-Problem Question that *offers choices* guarantees that both
you and your child will share in the decision making. If you
want to make sure your child comes up with the answer you
want, offer a Hobson's Choice — *unequal choices*. When you
do, in reality *you* decide the outcome.

INVOLVE YOUR CHILDREN IN DECISION MAKING

Whenever possible, involve your children in solving their
own problems and also family problems. Even small children,
for example, can help decide what to make for dinner. Older
children can help decide where to live or what house to buy.
You don't have to act on all their ideas, but simply including
children will make them feel their voices count and their ideas
are important to you. Whenever children are included they
are more likely to accept what you finally decide.

Also avoid being too quick to solve your children's problems for them. They must have time to try to handle them
themselves. Although they may need your help eventually,
jumping in too soon can make them reluctant to try to re-
solve things on their own. Whenever children solve their
problems with only the help they truly need, they grow more
confident. In addition, temporary failure can be a valuable
learning experience for them.

Consider the following two approaches to a problem
faced by my wife, Rotraud, when she baby-sat a friend's

children. Jenna and her brothers and sisters had been giving Rotraud quite a time. Their parents had gone away for a few days, and the children were testing our house rules. Every time she didn't have her way, Jenna would throw a temper tantrum. She constantly fought with her brothers and kept everything in an uproar.

At first, Rotraud tried to ignore her behavior. This is often a good strategy for dealing with unruly children, especially if the children are trying to attract attention. This approach didn't work this time. One day Jenna took all of her brother's crayons. Without Rotraud's knowledge of the Solve-The-Problem Question, the next step in resolving the situation might have gone like this:

CRAYONS SCENE #1

ROTRAUD: Jenna! What is the matter with you, young
lady? Give him back his crayons.

JENNA: Why should I? You're not my mother. I don't
have to do what you say.

ROTRAUD: Don't be rude. Go to your room.

JENNA: Why should I have to go? He started it.

ROTRAUD: I saw what happened. You took his crayons.
Now go to your room.

JENNA: (*stomps to her room, crying and protesting all
the way*) Just wait till my mom gets home.
I'm going to tell on you.

CRAYONS SCENE #2

Fortunately, Rotraud solved the crayon issue between Jenna and her brother by using Solve-The-Problem Questions to reach a much happier conclusion. Here's how it went:

ROTRAUD: Jenna, give him back his crayons. He had them first.

JENNA: Why should I? You're not my mother.

ROTRAUD: (*knowing time out would be helpful in avoiding further confrontation*) Go to your room. I'll be up in a few minutes, and we'll talk about this.

JENNA: I don't have to do what you say. You're not my boss.

ROTRAUD: Jenna, would you like to go up to your bedroom yourself, or do you want me to take you? (Solve-The-Problem Question — Hobson's Choice)

JENNA: Leave me alone! I'll go myself. (*She stomps off, crying and protesting.*) Just wait until my mom gets home. I'm telling on you.

Rotraud ignored this irrelevant behavior, waiting for Jenna to settle down in her room. Then she went upstairs to talk to her.

JENNA: Leave me alone. Go away.

ROTRAUD: Jenna, I can't go away or leave you alone because I love you and your brothers and sisters. I care about what's happening. Your mom and dad have asked me to look after you all. Without your help, that's very hard to do. What's wrong? (Tell-Me-What's-On-Your-Mind Question)

JENNA: (*shouting*) Nothing! Just leave me alone.

ROTRAUD: You're very upset. You miss your mom and dad, don't you? (Give-Me-Specific-Information Question)

JENNA: (*pausing to think about this for a moment*) I want my mom and dad.

ROTRAUD: I miss them too. They're my good friends. (Walk-In-Their-Shoes Statement) They will be gone for a few more days yet. We'll have to get along until then. If we are going to have some fun together and not fight all the time, I need your help, Jenna. What can we do about this? (Tell-Me-What's-On-Your-Mind Question)

JENNA: (*silence*)

ROTRAUD: I'm sorry you're so upset. I'm sure you don't want to be unhappy all the time until they get home, do you? (Give-Me-Specific-Information Question)

JENNA: (*thinks about this for a moment*) No.

ROTRAUD: Jenna, it will be three more days before your mom and dad are back. We can work together to get along till then, or we can keep on fighting. Which do you prefer? (Solve-The-Problem Question — Hobson's Choice)

JENNA: (*calmer now*) To get along.

ROTRAUD: Me too. You miss your mom and dad a lot. (Walk-In-Their-Shoes Statement) How can I help you feel better while they are gone? (Tell-Me-What's-On-Your-Mind Question)

JENNA: I don't know.

ROTRAUD: Jenna, you said you didn't like me being the boss. Could it be that you like to be in charge sometimes? (Give-Me-Specific-Information Question)

JENNA: (*with a smile appearing on her face*) No.

ROTRAUD: (*recognizing the smile as a reflex resulting from Jenna knowing the truth of what Rotraud has said, even though Jenna denied it*) Maybe things would go better if we worked together. You know more about how your mom and dad do things. Perhaps when you see me do something in a different way, you could help me by telling me how your mom and dad do it. We could try it that way. Maybe then you will feel more comfortable with my decisions. What do you think? Would you like to help me? (Give-Me-Specific-Information Question)

JENNA: Yes.

ROTRAUD: Good. Let's start now. I have to make dinner soon. What should we have?

Even though Jenna was just seven years old, she was able to see the problem she and Rotraud were having and to agree to help rather than to keep fighting. With the use of Tell-Me-What's-On-Your Mind and Give-Me-Specific-Information Questions, Rotraud was able to get Jenna to consider the problem and think about how they could solve it. Rotraud's use of the Solve-The-Problem Question let Jenna feel she had a choice. Jenna welcomed the chance to make some of the decisions. By allowing her to do so, Rotraud managed to change Jenna's attitude. In the end, everything ran more smoothly and everyone was happier. The Solve-The-Problem Question, even with unequal choices, helps children feel in control of their lives and gives them a chance to think and grow.

CHECKUP

The first step of the Solve-The-Problem Question is to _____. The second step is to either _____ or _____. Choices may be either _____, or _____, or _____. When the choices are unequal, the Solve-The-Problem Question is a _____.

Possible Answers:
define the problem, ask for possible solutions, offer choices, equal, limited, unequal, Hobson's Choice

HOBSON'S CHOICE

The dictionary says that a Hobson's Choice is "the choice of taking what is offered or nothing at all." It's not a real choice. It was named after Thomas Hobson (1544-1631) of Cambridge, England, who rented horses and gave his customers only one choice, that of the horse nearest the stable door. Hobson did this because the people who came to rent his horses always asked for the best one. As he had only two good horses, they were constantly rented and were being over-ridden, while the others stayed in the stable and got fat. He decided to change the way he gave customers horses.

Hobson numbered his horses and placed the No. 1 horse in the stall nearest the stable door. As soon as horse No. 1 went out, he replaced it with horse No. 2. Horses that had just been ridden were never put in the first stall, so they had time to rest. In this way Hobson rotated the use of each of his horses. Hence we have the term: Hobson's Choice.

12

"This Is The Deal . . ."

This-Is-The-Deal Statement (TTD)

This-Is-The-Deal Statements are another way to involve your child in finding solutions to problems. It asks, "If I do this, will you do that?" or it states, "If you do this, I will do that." In either case, you are making a deal with the child.

**This-Is-The-Deal
Statement**

Set up a contract with your child:

Step 1. Make a proposal about what one person will do (using the word "if" to begin the statement).

Step 2. State what is to be done by the other person in return.

Whatever follows the word "if" must be done first. Since both parent and child

---

must agree in order to make this work, it is an "Our Way" parenting approach.

Here's How

1. "If you'll get the bat and gloves, I'll play ball with you now." (requires the child to act first)
2. "If I help you put out the garbage, you can help me rake the leaves." (requires the parent to act first)

The way that you state a This-Is-The-Deal Statement depends on whom you think should act first — you or your child. Whether you or your child acts first depends on your judgment of whose action is more likely to get the result you desire.

For example, if you want your child to keep a tidy room and you believe that he or she will clean it up with little prompting, you might say, "If I make breakfast, will you straighten up your room?" On the other hand, if you feel uncertain of your child's willingness to straighten his or her room, you might say, "If you clean your room, I'll make break-fast." Use this "If you do this, I'll do that" approach if you feel you must get a promise from your child before you will perform your part of the deal.

Notice that you keep much of the decision-making control with the "If you do this, I'll do that" approach (the child acts first and you act second). You give more of the control to your child with the "If I do this, will you do that?" method. In either case, you decide who will act first (the action following the word "if").

Remember, the intent of a This-Is-The-Deal Statement is that you do something your child wants and your child does something you want.

Practice 1

In the following This-Is-The-Deal Statement, underline the part that gives the child something:

> PARENT: If I raise your allowance, will you baby-sit each Wednesday?

Answer:

If I raise your allowance

In the next This-Is-The-Deal Statement, underline the part that states what you expect your child to do:

> PARENT: If you'll take out the garbage each week, I'll raise your allowance by 25 cents.

Answer:

If you'll take out the garbage each week

Practice 2

For each This-Is-The-Deal Statement below, check whether the parent or the child needs to act first:

1. If I agree to take you fishing this weekend, will you help me clean up the garage next weekend?

___ Parent Acts First
___ Child Acts First

2. If you'll help me clean up the garage today, I can take you fishing next weekend.

___ Parent Acts First
___ Child Acts First

3. Yes, I'll help you fix your bike this afternoon if you'll rake the lawn this morning.

___ Parent Acts First
___ Child Acts First

4. If I help you fix your bike this afternoon, will you be sure to rake the leaves tomorrow?

___ Parent Acts First
___ Child Acts First

Answers:
1. Parent acts first, 2. Child acts first, 3. Child acts first, 4. Parent acts first

Notice that each time the "If . . . then . . ." ends in a question, the parent acts first. It's hard to make anyone do something after they have gotten what they want. You need to make the child promise to carry out his or her part of the bargain. If there is any doubt about that, make sure the child understands that his or her part of the contract (and this *is* a contract) must happen first.

DEFINITE AND SUGGESTED BARGAINS

There is another way to state a This-Is-The-Deal Statement to make sure your child will act first. Instead of saying, "If you do this, I'll do that," you might say, "After you do this, you *may be able to* do that." In the first approach, you make a *definite* bargain with your child. In the second, you only *suggest* a bargain.

The following example more clearly shows the difference between these two forms of This-Is-The-Deal Statements. As a *definite* bargain, you might word the This-Is-The-Deal Statement in the following way:

PARENT: If you finish your homework on time, I'll take you to the game.

As a *suggested* bargain, you could state the This-Is-The-Deal Statement this way:

PARENT: After you finish your homework, you may get to come to the game with me.

The second case, using the word "may," states a *suggested* bargain between parent and child. The child's action follows the word "after." Therefore, the parent *suggests* cooperation with the words, "you may." The parent *may not* take the child to the game if, for example, the child takes too long to get the homework done and it's then too late to get to the game on time. The parent hasn't broken his or her word, because the bargain allowed for the possibility that the deal might not work out. *If you doubt the outcome, suggest a bargain.*

Practice 3

Keep in mind that, as with the other communication skills, you must state the This-Is-The-Deal Statement positively. Say, "I will do this if you do that." Avoid saying, "I won't do this if you don't do that."

To make sure you understand how to handle positive phrasing, consider the examples below. In the space after each negatively phrased This-Is-The-Deal Statement, write a positive one:

> PARENT: I won't drive you to work until you put the clean dishes away.

_____

_____

Possible Answers:
"If you put the clean dishes away, I'll drive you to work."
"If I drive you to work, will you put the clean dishes away before supper?"

> PARENT: If you two don't stop this fighting while you play, I'll put you in separate rooms.

_____

_____

Possible Answers:
"If I let you play together, will you get along with each other?"
"If you make an effort to get along with each other, I'll let you play together."

PARENT: If you don't start getting home on time, I'll start dinner without you.

_____

_____

Possible Answers:
"If I have dinner ready, will you be home on time?"
"I'll have dinner ready if you are home on time."
"If you are home before 5:30, I'll have dinner ready and
   waiting for you."

Practice 4

Now try some This-Is-The-Deal Statements of your own. In the spaces following the descriptions of the various situations, write an appropriate This-Is-The-Deal Statement in which either you or your child take the first action.

Your daughter wants to buy a toy. She usually knows the value of money. Unfortunately, she does not have enough money saved to buy the toy she wants, and this is the last day it's on sale. She pleads, "Please lend me the money. I promise I'll pay it back." You think she should earn the money.

Parent Takes First Action:

_____

_____

Child Takes First Action:

_____

_____

Possible Answers:
If you feel the child will keep her word, you could say, "If I
give you the dollar you need now, will you earn it by
helping me clean the windows this afternoon?"
On the other hand, if you think she might have trouble
keeping the bargain, you might say, "If you help me
clean the windows this morning, I'll pay you the dollar
you need for your toy."

Let's look at another situation: Your child objects to doing
any chores, saying, "Why do I have to do everything?"

Parent Takes First Action:

_____

_____

Child Takes First Action:

_____

_____

Possible Answers:
If you are sure enough of your child's response, you could
say, "If I let you go without doing your chores for a
whole week, will you agree that I can do the same thing
myself the next week?"

If you were less confident, you would want to make sure your child performed his or her part of the bargain first. Then you might say, "If you let me go for a week without doing any chores, then I'll let you go for a week without doing any." (A parent we know took this approach with her son, who refused to help her when she asked him. Because of his refusal to help, he found no meals prepared, no ride to judo class, no help in repairing his bike chain, and no help with his homework. He got the message! He soon discovered why he needed to do his share of the chores.)

Here's one final example: Your son begs to go swimming and he is to take a nap.

Parent Takes First Action:

_____

_____

Child Takes First Action:

_____

_____

Possible Answers:
A This-Is-The-Deal Statement in which you act first might sound like this: "I will take you swimming now, if you will take a nap as soon as we get back."
If you want to have your child act first, try this response: "If you will take your nap now, I will take you when you wake up."

A This-Is-The-Deal Statement, like the Solve-The-Problem Question that offers equal options, lets your child make some of the decisions. This-Is-The-Deal Statements promise that you will both act. You are making a contract with your child.

In the following example, notice how one mother might have used This-Is-The-Deal Statements to handle a problem she was having. Her son Ahron had left the car he was restoring in her driveway. He had moved out some time earlier and not taken the car away as he had been asked to do. The parents were moving soon and had to have the car off the property. The mother was especially worried because Ahron was about to leave town to take part in a training program.

First, see how she handled her problem without using This-Is-The-Deal Statements:

MOTHER: (*on the phone to her son*) Ahron, you've got to move your car this week.

AHRON: (*clearly frustrated*) How can I? I've got to leave tomorrow. I've got a million things to do first. Besides, where am I going to put it?

MOTHER: I told you before. Art will let you store it at his place. I want it out of here tomorrow.

AHRON: I don't have any money to have it towed.

MOTHER: That's your problem. It's your car.

AHRON: And I've got too much to do. I have to leave for training tomorrow. I want to see Rebecca this afternoon.

MOTHER: (*exasperated*) I told you a year ago the car had to be moved. It's still there. I'm sick and tired of asking you to move it.

AHRON: (*angrier*) What am I supposed to do now?

TIME FOR TOWING

MOTHER: If you don't look after it today, I'll get it towed to the wreckers.

AHRON: Fine! I don't care. Do what ever you want. Goodbye!

No winners here. Mother and son both lost: the car is still sitting in Mother's driveway and Ahron is about to lose a car he really wants to rebuild. She is angry and frustrated, and he feels angry and pressured. While he may be in the wrong, he doesn't care. Clearly, she should have made sure he moved the car a year ago. She didn't, and the way she is handling the problem is just making him angry.

What is needed is a way to handle the situation that will satisfy both of them. Here is how she might have handled it using This-Is-The-Deal Statements:

MOTHER: *(on the phone to her son)* Ahron, you've got to move your car this week.

AHRON: *(clearly frustrated)* How can I? I've got to leave tomorrow for my course. I've got a million things to do. I don't have time. Besides, where am I going to put it?

MOTHER: *(calmly showing she understands and providing additional information)* I'm sorry you're under a lot of pressure right now. The car must be taken away before we move. The landlord won't let me leave it here.

AHRON: Where am I going to put it?

MOTHER: You certainly have a problem. I asked Art, and he said you can leave the car on his lot until you can make other arrangements. You just have to get it towed there.

AHRON: I don't have any money for the towing. I don't get paid until after the course. How am I going to pay for it?

MOTHER: If you will have it towed today, I will lend you the money and you can pay me back. (This-Is-The-Deal Statement)

AHRON: But I don't have time! I want to see Rebecca before I go, and I'm still not packed.

MOTHER: I'm sorry you have so much to do. I have to pack, and I don't have time either. If you call Gray's, I know they will move it today.

AHRON: Can't you call them?

MOTHER: Calling is your responsibility. If you call and have them come this afternoon, I can give

them a check. (This-Is-The-Deal Statement)
You will have to talk to Art too.

AHRON: I'm swamped.

MOTHER: If we get off the phone now, you can call
Gray's. (This-Is-The-Deal Statement) You can
also let Art know the car is coming. If you
call both right now, the car will be there
when you get back. If you wait until it's too
late, the landlord will have the car towed and
you will have to pay a lot more to get it back.
I don't have the time either.

AHRON: Okay! I'll get it moved.

MOTHER: Thank you. If you take care of it today, I'll
give the driver the check when he comes.
(This-Is-The-Deal Statement) Then your car
will be safe until you can work on it again.

While Ahron is still not happy that he has yet another
job to do before he leaves, he is less frustrated. His mother
clearly showed she knew how he felt. She also made a deal
with Ahron to make it easier for him to afford to have it towed
now. Moreover, the deal she made placed the responsibility
where it belonged, on Ahron. In the end, they resolved the
problem and kept their relationship positive.

A This-Is-The-Deal Statement is a way of making a _____ with your child. In this two-step skill, you make a proposal about _____. Then you state what _____.

Possible Answers:
contract, what one person will do, is to be done by the other person in return

Now that you have a clear understanding of *how* and *when* to use This-Is-The-Deal Statements, turn to the next problem-solving and decision-making skill, the Out-Of-Bounds Statement.

13

"That's Out of Bounds!"

Out-Of-Bounds Statement
(OB)

*S*ometimes parents must disapprove. It can be difficult to do this and still support your child. Parents often say things they later regret. When you disapprove of what your children do, use statements such as the following:

> PARENT 1: Your room is too messy for you to have friends visit.
>
> PARENT 2: You must read the instructions carefully if the model is to fly.

Avoid phrases such as these:

> PARENT 1: Can't you keep your room tidy? We're having company.
>
> PARENT 2: What's the matter with you? Can't you follow simple instructions?

Remarks like these immediately make your children defensive. That is because such comments criticize the child

223

rather than disapprove of the child's actions (or lack of actions). When parents criticize children in front of others, especially their friends or their brothers or sisters, the children tend to gang up on the parents. When parents criticize one child, the other children feel threatened as well and usually support each other.

You need to be less personal. The Out-Of-Bounds Statement can prevent the children from banding together against the parent.

Examples of the Out-Of-Bounds Statement:

PARENT 1: Your homework is too messy to read.
PARENT 2: That talking is bothering us.
PARENT 3: I'm upset that you've come home late. You had me very worried.

With each of these Out-Of-Bounds Statements, the parent disapproves of the child's *actions*, but does not make the child feel personally attacked.

**Out-Of-Bounds
Statement**

Step 1. Determine what actions are unacceptable.
Step 2. Disapprove of the child's actions, not the child.
This is a "My Way" skill.

Here's How

1. "Throwing stones at other children can hurt them."
2. "Leaving your shoes in the doorway could cause an accident."
3. "Dishes are hard to wash if they're left overnight on the counter."
4. "When you left the car lights on, the battery ran down."
5. "Leaving your toys on the sidewalk overnight led to the neighbor running over them."

Look at the following statements. Which are good Out-Of-Bounds Statements?

1. ____ "What a stupid thing to do!"

2. ____ "Taking what doesn't belong to you is against the law."

3. ____ "Your handwriting is awful."

4. ____ "You bully! Pick on someone your own size!"

5. ____ "While you're talking, I can't hear Alexander speak."

Answer:
Nos. 2 and 5 are positively phrased examples of Out-Of-Bounds Statements.

FOCUS ON THE ACT INSTEAD OF THE ACTOR

With the Out-Of-Bounds Statement, you *focus on the act, not on the actor*. You aim your criticism at the children's problem behavior and you avoid criticizing your children themselves. For example, focus on the untidy room, the loud radio, or the dangerous play.

Deciding what actions are unacceptable is the first step of the Out-Of-Bounds Statement. The second step is to state this disapproval in such a way that your children understand you are criticizing the act, not them personally. An angry parent might strike out with the words "Taking that toy was mean." You'd think the parent was criticizing only the child's act, but that's not so. The word "mean" describes people, not actions. The parent has really said the *child* is mean.

Parents need to take a different approach. For example, you might say:

> PARENT: Taking other people's things without their
>   consent upsets them. I can't let you take
>   other children's toys without asking first.

Consider this fact: Children can change the way they *act*, they cannot change who they *are*. In *Being the Parent YOU Want to Be*, we call words such as "mean," "stupid," "dumb," "ridiculous," "dishonest," and so forth, "slob words." When parents use these words, children think their parents mean that *the children*, rather than the children's actions, are dumb, ridiculous, or dishonest. Only a person can be stupid. Slob words harm children's fragile egos more than most parents realize.

For example, here is a parent shouting at his children for roughhousing in the living room:

PARENT: What are you, wise guys? Stop that wrestling. You'll break something with your stupid horseplay.

The parent attacked the children personally with the slob words "wise guys" and "stupid." This could convince them they actually are "wise guys" and "stupid." They might not have thought of themselves this way before the parent pinned these labels on them.

Here is a better way to disapprove of the children's roughhousing inside:

PARENT: Wrestling in the living room is dangerous. Someone could get hurt. Go outside and wrestle on the lawn.

This Out-Of-Bounds Statement focuses on the children's actions, not on the children themselves. Now they understand why the parent stopped the roughhousing. They hear no slob words, neither do they feel personally attacked. Now they do not have to live up to a negative image.

Practice 1

Here are some Out-Of-Bounds Statements. After each one, circle whether it is a good or poor statement. Briefly explain the reason why you think so.

PARENT: Your boots are too muddy to wear in the house. Take them off.

Good   Poor

Possible Answer:

This is a good Out-Of-Bounds Statement. It focuses on the muddy boots, not on any of the child's personal attributes, and it tells the child what you want done.

> PARENT: You've behaved irresponsibly. I don't know what I'm going to do with you.
>
> Good   Poor

Possible Answer:

This is a poor Out-Of-Bounds Statement. People, not acts, are irresponsible. The parent might better have said something like this: "You should have turned the stove off when you went outside. After we review the safety rules, you can use the stove again."

> PARENT: Your radio is bothering everyone in the house. Turn it down or take it outside and listen to it there.
>
> Good   Poor

Possible Answer:

This is a good Out-Of-Bounds Statement. It states that the radio is bothersome, not the child.

> PARENT: That was a hateful thing to do! How could you dump sand on her head?
>
> Good   Poor

Possible Answer:

People are hateful, acts are not — although acts may hurt others. This is a poor Out-Of-Bounds Statement. A better statement would be: "Dumping sand on Mary's head has hurt her. The sand got into her eyes."

PARENT: Only stupid people smoke marijuana.

Good   Poor

Possible Answer:

This is a poor Out-Of-Bounds Statement, attacking the child, not the behavior.

Practice 2

Now write some Out-Of-Bounds Statements of your own. First read each of the following situations, then write your answers in the spaces below. Remember, concentrate on the child's *act* and why you disapprove of it. Avoid criticizing the child, especially by using slob words.

You have just discovered that your child has taken money from your drawer without asking. Write your Out-Of-Bounds Statement in the space provided:

_____

_____

Possible Answers:

"You know taking money that isn't yours is against our family rules."

"Taking money out of my drawer without asking first makes me angry."

"You'll feel better if you earn your own money. I do when I work hard for something I want."

Notice the above responses avoid words such as "dishonest," "stealing," and "thief." Again, these slob words apply only to people, not to actions.

In the next example, your child has broken a window. Write your Out-Of-Bounds Statement in the space below:

_____

_____

Possible Answers:

"Now that the window is broken, you'll have to replace it
   with new glass."

"Breaking the window means we must buy new glass.
   That's expensive."

"The rain will get in now that the window is broken."

Here, too, the parent avoids slob words such as "irresponsible," "careless," and "stupid," so the child doesn't feel the need to be defensive.

The final example has your child teasing a neighbor's children. Write your Out-Of-Bounds Statement to address this problem in the space below:

_____

_____

Possible Answers:

"You upset them with your teasing."

"Your teasing remarks hurt their feelings."

"Kind remarks would encourage them to play with you."

The best Out-Of-Bounds Statements suggest alternatives that will create a desired change in your child's actions. For this reason, the Out-Of-Bounds Statement is a "My Way" approach to parenting. Even the most permissive parent will use Out-Of-Bounds Statements from time to time.

TO SUM UP

By directing your disapproval solely at the children's actions, without name calling, you avoid the possibility that children will make connections between themselves and the acts of which you disapprove.

CHECKUP

The _____ is a _____ approach to parenting. With it, you direct your disapproval solely at your child's _____. You must always avoid the use of _____ that may encourage your child to act out the behavior you have criticized. The best Out-Of-Bounds Statement helps create a _____ change in your child's actions by suggesting alternatives.

Possible Answers:
Out-Of-Bounds Statement, "my way," actions, slob words, positive

"Do It!"

Do-It-This-Way Statement (DITW)

*T*he last of the *12 Communication Skills for Effective Parenting* is the Do-It-This-Way Statement. The Do-It-This-Way Statement is a "My Way" approach to parenting you can use every day to give directions and instructions to your children. Here's an example:

> PARENT: Children, the ball you are throwing might break a window. Please move your game to the other side of the yard.

With the Do-It-This-Way Statement, you tell children why they are to do something, and you avoid scolding. For example, if you were to simply say to your child, "Wash your dish again," without an explanation, you might very well find yourself having to repeat the instruction again and again. When you make clear *why* your child must rewash the dish, your child is more likely to do the job right the next time without a reminder. It is very important that your explanation

233

be clear and brief — avoid lecturing! Lecturing makes children "parent deaf."

Do-It-This-Way
Statement

Step 1. State what you want done.
Step 2. Give the reason.
Either step:
- May come first.
- May be implied.

Your statement will be correct if it tells the child *why* you want something done. This is another "My Way" parenting approach.

Here's How

1. "Bring enough to eat. We'll be hiking all day."
2. "They won't let you into the restaurant with bare feet. Put your shoes on."
3. "Turn the stove off when you're finished cooking." (reason implied)

The Do-It-This-Way Statement requires two steps. The first step is to *say what you want done*. The second step is to *state clearly why you want it done*. If the reason why you are asking the child to do something is obvious, you may wish to only *imply* the second step. For example:

PARENT: Throw the darts *away from* the dance floor.

In this Do-It-This-Way Statement, the reason for doing what you asked is clear — dancers may be hurt by flying darts. Whenever the reason is quite clear, you need only imply it. Even so, you could have explained your reason by saying something like this:

> PARENT: If you throw the darts near the dance floor, you might hurt someone. Throw them at the dartboard in the other room.

The order of the two steps could also be reversed. In that case, your statement might be something like this:

> PARENT: Take the darts and throw them in the other room. You might hurt someone by throwing them near the dance floor.

Here the "why" comes *after* the command. Whether the reason for doing something comes before or after the command is unimportant. As long as your child knows the reason for your directive, even if you only imply it, your Do-It-This-Way Statement will be effective. If there is any doubt about whether your child understands why you are issuing your orders, give the reason.

Practice 1

Now let's practice what you have learned about the Do-It-This-Way Statement. For each situation described below, phrase a suitable Do-It-This-Way Statement. Use your good judgment about whether or not to use both steps or imply the reason. Whatever you decide, the child should clearly understand your reason for telling him or her to do something.

In the first example, your young child is constantly pulling on your arm. She keeps demanding that you stop reading the paper and read her a story.

_____

_____

Possible Answers:
"Please wait until I finish the paper, then I will read
    to you. Tugging on my arm bothers me." (reason
    given after)
"Please wait until I finish the paper." (reason implied)
"I can't read the paper while you're tugging on my arm.
    Please wait until I finish." (reason given first)

Next, some children are making too much noise in the driveway. You have been trying to sleep after your night shift at work.

_____

_____

Possible Answers:
"Children, please be quiet. I worked all night, and your
    noise is keeping me from sleeping." (reason given)
"I'm trying to sleep after working the night shift. Please go
    somewhere else to play. You're welcome to come back
    later." (reason given)
"Children, please be quiet out there." (reason implied —
    children know parent is sleeping)

This time, one of your children has been using your tools and has left them outside in the rain.

_____

_____

Possible Answers:
"It's upsetting to find my tools in the rain. Dry them off and put them away so they won't rust." (reason given)
"Bring the tools in, dry them off, and put them away where they belong." (reason implied)
"Dry off my tools and put them away. I need them put away so I can find them the next time I need them. And I don't want them to rust." (reasons given)

Finally, tell them how to hold a family fire drill.

_____

_____

Possible Answers:
"Children, it's important that everyone knows what to do in case of a fire. When you hear the alarm, roll out of bed and crawl to the door, feel if it's hot . . . ." (reason given)
"You know how we handle fire alarms. Here is what to do . . . ." (reason given)
"When you hear the fire alarm buzzer, immediately . . . ." (reason implied)

CHECKUP

The Do-It-This-Way Statement works well when you need to tell your children to do something. Use the Do-It-This-Way Statement whenever you direct, instruct, or require something of your children.

The Do-It-This-Way Statement has two steps. The first is to _____ and the second is to _____. The first step of the Do-It-This-Way Statement may be _____ when the reasons for telling children what to do are _____. The two steps may also be _____. Whenever you are in doubt that your children know why you tell them to do something, include both steps.

Possible Answers:
state what you want them to do, give reasons, implied, obvious, reversed

15

You've Learned a Lot!

*Y*ou now know how to use the four Skills for Solving Problems and Making Decisions With Your Child. Each offers different amounts of decision-making control. When you ask for solutions to a problem with a broad Solve-The-Problem Question, for example, you give your children control over how the problem will be solved. You share the decision whenever a Solve-The-Problem Question asks for solutions or gives limited or equal choices. You also share decision-making control when you offer a This-Is-The-Deal Statement.

On the other hand, you keep control of the decision-making process when your Solve-The-Problem Question is a Hobson's Choice offering unequal choices. You also keep control whenever you use an Out-Of-Bounds Statement or a Do-It-This-Way Statement.

Clearly, the first problem-solving and decision-making skill that you have learned, the Solve-The-Problem Question, gives you the greatest range of control. How much you let the child get involved depends upon whether you ask for solutions or offer them. It also depends on how you state the problem in the first place.

Consider this Solve-The-Problem Question:

PARENT: We decided about how to act in the car. Would you like to follow the rules and continue on to the circus or stay home with a sitter?

This Solve-The-Problem Question is a Hobson's Choice. Presumably, the children would prefer going to the circus. If so, the children have:

    ____   Unlimited choices.
    ____   Limited, but equal choices.
    ____   No real choice at all.
    ____   Two equally desirable alternatives.

Answer:
No real choice at all. (The children know the rules. If they do not want to behave in the car, the only other choice is a sitter.)

Whenever a Solve-The-Problem Question offers children unequal choices (a Hobson's Choice), there's no real choice at all. The decision:

    ____   Belongs to the parent.
    ____   Rests with the child.
    ____   Rests with both equally.

Answer:
Belongs to the parent.

The second problem-solving and decision-making communication skill you have learned, the This-Is-The-Deal Statement, requires both the parent *and* the child to do something. Even so, the parent decides how much of the decision will be shared with the child. For example, consider the following This-Is-The-Deal Statements:

1. If each of you will tell me what you want to see on our vacation, I'll make sure we go to as many of these places as we have time for.

2. If each of you will tell me what you want to see on our vacation, then I'll listen to your choices and pick the ones that will be the most fun for the money and time we have.

Each of the above This-Is-The-Deal Statements limits the children's control because:

_____   The parent gives the children limited choices.
_____   The parent lets the children make all of the decisions.

Answer:
The parent gives the children limited choices.

The third problem-solving and decision-making communication skill you have learned is the Out-Of-Bounds Statement. Out-Of-Bounds Statements contain a solution to a problem and tell your children how you want them to change the way they act. Consider this example:

PARENT: Your bed isn't made.

In this Out-Of-Bounds Statement, the parent implies what he or she expects the child to do: the child must make the bed. The decision about what is to be done in this Out-Of-Bounds Statement is made by:

_____   The child.
_____   The parent.
_____   Both parent and child.

Answer:
The parent.

The final problem-solving and decision-making communication skill you have learned is the Do-It-This-Way Statement. The Do-It-This-Way Statement makes the solution to a problem obvious. For example:

PARENT: It's clear you're not willing to stay out of the street when playing outside. You are to stay in the house for the rest of the morning.

In the above Do-It-This-Way Statement, the parent:

_____   Kept control of the decision.
_____   Shared the decision making with the child.
_____   Gave the decision making to the child.

Answer:
Kept control of the decision.

CHECKUP

All of the Skills for Solving Problems and Making Decisions With Your Child (except the Out-Of-Bounds Statement) are two-step strategies. The Out-Of-Bounds Statement has only one step: direct _____ solely at the child's _____. The first step of the Solve-The-Problem Question is to _____. The second step is to ask for _____ or offer _____. The possible solutions may request a range of answers that are _____, _____, or _____. The choices can be _____, _____, or _____. When you provide an unequal choice, you are offering your child a _____.

In This-Is-The-Deal Statements, decide if you or your child will _____, depending upon which way is more likely to produce the results you want. Then offer the child your deal. First, _____ and second, state _____. What should be done first follows the word _____.

Possible Answers:
disapproval, actions or behavior, define the problem, possible solutions, choices, broad, narrow, very narrow, equal, limited, unequal, Hobson's Choice, take the first action, make a proposal about what one person will do, what is to be done by the other person, if

BRIDGE BUILDING

You now have many effective ways to help your child make decisions and solve problems. Try to use each problem-solving skill at least three times during the coming week. Note why you used one skill instead of another to solve a problem. Again, you might want to use a special notebook to record your thoughts and experiences. Note, too, your children's responses. When using the Solve-The-Problem Question, pay particular attention to your children's responses when *you* limit the choices instead of offering equal choices. Is there a difference when you offer unequal, few, or many choices? Watch how other people use them.

When possible, use the Solve-The-Problem Question and This-Is-The-Deal Statement rather than the Do-It-This-Way and the Out-Of-Bounds Statements. While these latter communication skills are important, they have limited use; they should be used only when parents must take quick action. Do-It-This-Way Statements and Out-Of-Bounds Statements do not help children learn to solve their own problems. Your children will become more responsibly independent when you stress the Solve-The-Problem Question and This-Is-The-Deal Statement.

After you have done this for a week, reread Part 4: "What WILL We Do?" — Solving Problems and Making Decisions With Your Child. Doing this will help you use these communication skills naturally and automatically.

FOOD FOR THOUGHT

Long-term rules, chores, and routines are the easiest to get children to follow. Short-term rules or commands are more difficult to get children to pay attention to. Parents usually try to get children to do something through commands or disapproval of problem behavior.

CREATIVE WAYS TO SOLVE PROBLEMS

In the remainder of this chapter, we will look at creative ways some parents have used to help their children solve problems and take responsibility. While our focus is on the problem-solving and decision-making communication skills, many of the other communication skills you've learned in this book are used to show more clearly what actually took place.

All parents and children need to solve problems and make decisions. Parents face a variety of issues every day. Ideally, parents and children will work together to handle them, and in doing so, children learn from parents responsible ways of handling life's problems and opportunities. Let's see how some parents have used the problem-solving and decision-making skills to solve the day-to-day problems that arise in every home.

Remember earlier, while playing in a sandbox, one child dumped a shovelful of sand on another child's head. Here's what Jennifer's mother said:

> "Jennifer, stop putting sand on Mary's head.
> The sand gets into her eyes and hurts her."
> (Do-It-This-Way Statement)

Here's how other parents handled difficult situations:

> "Juanita, throwing your garbage on the ground is
> littering. Your lunch trash belongs in the garbage can."
> (Do-It-This-Way Statement)

> "I can't hear when you have the television set so loud."
> (Do-It-This-Way Statement)

> "Robert, the police delivered a summons for you
> today. You forgot to pay your traffic ticket. Now you
> have to go to court. When you started to drive, we

agreed that if you got a ticket you could not use the car until you paid the ticket and we renewed our understanding. (This-Is-The-Deal Statement) So when you have cleared this up, we will talk about when you may use the car again." (Do-It-This-Way Statement)

Notice that in the situation with Robert the parent did not add to the punishment, but held to agreements established when Robert first began to drive. Robert will not only have to go to court and pay a fine, he will also not drive the car again until he and his parent go back over the ground rules. The parent did not have to explain the obvious.

"The dirty dishes were left in the sink after your party. I brought company home after work and the mess embarrassed me." (Out-Of-Bounds Statement)

The disapproval here, as it should always be, is directed solely at the *act*, not at the child. Assuming the child and parent have an otherwise good relationship, you should not have to say any more, except perhaps to tell the child to clean up the dishes. The parent, despite the embarrassment, was wise not to do the child's job. Parents need to be more concerned about teaching their children to be responsible than about what others think of them as parents.

INVOLVING CHILDREN IN PROBLEM SOLVING

Problem-solving training should start as soon as children can think. Even newborns can be encouraged to begin problem solving. In fact, they start solving problems from the moment they are born.

Parents more often use the Solve-The-Problem Question with older children. Consider the following examples.

Sometimes the parents ask children for solutions; sometimes they offer equal choices; and sometimes they give their children unequal choices.

In the first instance, Juan was sitting in front of his computer, looking wistfully out his bedroom window:

"What are you doing, Juan?" his father asked. (Give-Me-Specific-Information Question)

"Oh, nothing," Juan replied sheepishly.

"You have a keyboarding assignment due tomorrow, don't you?" (Give-Me-Specific-Information Question)

"Yes."

"Would you like to get back to it now or during the football game?" (Solve-The-Problem Question)

Juan, a dedicated football fan, replied to this Hobson's Choice: "I'll do it now."

"When you've finished," his father added, "show it to me. Then we can watch the game together." (Do-It-This-Way Statement)

In many households, bedtime and bath time are sources of considerable struggle between parent and child. Here's a solution I found in a book I read some years ago. The writer gave some good advice: "Never tell a child about upcoming disaster." For many children, bath time — and especially bedtime — spell what seems to them like disaster. Often this happens at the end of a fun-filled day. Instead of telling children they are about to have a bath or go to bed, try this:

"Erica, you've had a lot of fun today. You've gotten dirty. Tomorrow we're going to the fair. Would you like to get into your bath yourself, or would you like me to lift you in?" (Solve-The-Problem Question — Hobson's Choice)

Or, "Children, if you put your pajamas on and get yourselves into bed, I'll have time to read you a story." (This-Is-The-Deal Statement)

Both of these statements give children a choice only about *how* they will get into the bath or get ready for bed, not whether they will. Since story time is welcome in many households, children are usually willing to put their pajamas on and get into bed to hear their favorite story. As for climbing into the bath, most children say, "I'd rather do it myself."

In our house, had we asked our children if they wanted to have a bath or get into bed, they would have balked at either choice. But when asked in the ways suggested above, *they* made the decision.

SMALL PROBLEMS TO ADULTS,
LARGE PROBLEMS TO CHILDREN

What adults consider small problems are often big problems for children. Keeping up with what's "in" among their friends is one of those problems because children care what their friends think of them. When children ask for the latest fad clothes, for example, the parent-child relationship is better served by involving children in the decision making than by the parent simply saying "No." Here's how one parent solved the problem:

"Mom, I've got to get new running shoes. Can I get Dashers like Chan's?" Andrew asked eagerly.

"First we'll find out how much I can pay for your running shoes. If you don't like the brand I can afford, you can pay the difference and get the Dashers you want." (Do-It-this-Way Statement)

Having already decided that Andrew could have new running shoes, his mother wisely allowed Andrew to make his own decision about what brand he would get. Immediately saying "No" to Chan's brand would only have aroused Andrew's resistance.

After checking out the shoes at the mall and realizing how much extra he'd have to pay, Andrew chose the cheaper ones. His sister, faced with the same problem, chose the more expensive brand and paid the difference. They each decided and were happy with their choices. Andrew had more money left and his sister had the shoes she wanted. Their mother never became the "bad guy."

INCLUDE CHILDREN IN PLANNING

Here is an old saying that applies: "I see and I forget. I do and I remember." Children usually learn best by doing. Whenever possible, as families make plans that affect them, children should be part of that planning.

Each summer my friend's children go to camp. There are many things to do and many things have to be packed. My friend does most of the packing because her children are young (five and seven). She does, however, let the children do what they can. Here is what she does:

"Deborah and Stephen, we have to get you ready for camp this weekend. The bus leaves early Monday morning. After supper, I want you both to sit with me

PLANNING FOR CAMP

and make your lists for camp." (Do-It-This-Way Statement — this was not a request.)

From experience, the children already knew that not helping with the lists could mean no camp at all. If they wanted to go, they had to help with the plans. At ages five and seven, respectively, Stephen and Deborah had helped their mother make lists before. Now let's look in on their list-making. Pen in hand, Carol sat down at the kitchen table with the children and began:

"What activities are listed for camp this summer?" (Give-Me-Specific-Information Question)

In rapid-fire fashion, one after the other, the children responded enthusiastically:

"Swimming."

"Hiking."

"Crafts."

"Volleyball."

"Baseball."

On they went until they named them all.

"What will you need to participate in each of these activities?" Carol asked. (Tell-Me-What's-On-Your-Mind Question)

"We'll need our bathing suits and towels," Deborah chirped. "And we'll need to take sunblock and our running shoes."

"I'll have to take my baseball mitt," added Stephen.

"Me too!" Deborah shouted.

"Speak softly," her mother commanded. "You are hurting my ears." (Do-It-This-Way Statement)

"What will your personal needs be?" she asked.

"We'll need our shorts and T-shirts, flashlights, hair brushes, toothbrushes and toothpaste . . . and my hamster," declared Stephen.

Immediately Deborah corrected him: "No pets allowed at camp!"

"That's right," Carol said. "The brochure said 'No Pets.' You're not to take your Walkman® either." (Do-It-This-Way Statement)

They continued going through the various activities and what the children would need to have with them. Soon each child's list was complete. Then, giving Deborah her list and Stephen his, Carol said:

"First thing tomorrow, after breakfast, when you've dressed and straightened up your rooms, start putting the things from your lists onto your beds. (Do-It-This-Way Statement) When you get everything checked off, I will come to each of your rooms, and we can pack your camping gear." (This-Is-The-Deal Statement)

Carol then made sure the children knew what they could or couldn't take. She also made each one responsible for getting his or her own belongings together. If they had missed anything, they would find out about it together as they and Carol checked things off each list.

As they went through this process each summer, the children became more and more responsible for doing what had to be done. In time, they learned to make sure that every item on their lists was packed. Whenever a list was not carefully checked, the children, not their mother, lived with the results. And every time they made a mistake, they learned an important lesson.

By learning to think and plan for themselves, children will become responsible, independent adults.

ALLOW RECOVERY TIME

Sometimes when children run into obstacles, they simply need time to get over their frustrations. One mother in my Personalized Parenting course reported that she let time solve a problem for her:

> "It was Saturday afternoon, and I was trying to get my three-year-old daughter ready for company who had arrived while she was having her nap. No matter which outfit I got out for her, she refused to wear it. I tried everything I had learned in our first session of Personalized Parenting, but nothing worked. Samantha just got more upset until finally she became hysterical. In desperation, I said to her, 'You're very angry. (Walk-In-Their-Shoes Statement) Nothing I get out for you to wear makes you happy. (What-You-Meant Statement) I'm sorry you're so upset. (Walk-In-Their-Shoes Statement) If you want, you can stay here and have a good cry. Then, when you feel better, let me know and I'll come and get you.' (This-Is-The-Deal Statement)

> "Samantha was having a tantrum and I didn't know why. Since nothing helped, I decided to recognize her feelings and leave her to them. It worked. After only a few minutes, she called out from her bedroom, 'I finished now, Mommy.'

> "When I went back into her room, she had stopped crying. 'I better now, Mommy,' she said.

> "'Do you want to put on this new dress I bought you, or do you want to wear another one?' (Solve-The-Problem Question — equal options)

"'No! I wear this,' she said, holding up a pair of play-worn shorts.

"Realizing that wearing her old familiar shorts was important to her, I agreed. Apparently, she needed to wear something familiar right now (something I realized during the cooling-off period). Now we were both happy. Accepting my daughter's feelings and giving her time to deal with them worked for both of us. Sometimes it's better to let children decide for themselves."

ALLOW TIME FOR DECISION MAKING

Allowing sometimes irresponsible children to make decisions is often difficult, but parents *can* offer at least some decision-making responsibility to their children. The communication skills in each section work well with most children, and are meant to develop decision-making and problem-solving abilities *over time*. You can use them with even not-so-responsible children. Consider this next parent's experience as she shared it with my weekly parents' group:

"Julia was often a handful," Marie announced to the group. "Until I attended a Personalized Parenting workshop, I couldn't get her to do much of anything without a major battle. Things are different now. It's not as hard as I thought."

Everyone was anxious to hear what had caused Marie's enthusiasm for the program, so I encouraged her to continue.

"My Julia is 13. She loves dancing. At her school they were having the first seniors' dance for eighth graders. Julia really wanted to go, but she hadn't cleaned her room as she was supposed to.

"I saw this as a chance to let her decide and take some responsibility, so I decided to try the problem-solving skills. I was also hoping we might avoid a fight.

"When Julia asked me about the dance, I asked her about cleaning her room. 'Aw c'mon, Mom. I can do it Saturday.'

"'You feel I should let you do it Saturday, when you haven't done it all week.' (Think-It-Over Statement)

"'I'll do it, I promise.'

"'If you clean your room before dinner, I'll let you go to the dance,' I said. (This-Is-The-Deal Statement)

"'But Mom, I've got to get ready. I won't have time,' she said in that whiny voice I hate.

"'I know you have a lot to do to get ready,' I said. (Walk-In-Their-Shoes Statement) 'Your room was to be cleaned yesterday. (Support-Their-Thinking Statement — additional information) If you get it done before dinner, you can go to the dance,' I repeated. (This-Is-The-Deal Statement) Then I shut up! Usually I tell her more than she wants to hear. This time I just kept quiet and waited.

"'I can't. It's too messy. I'll do it Saturday.'

"I still said nothing. I just waited. Let me tell you, *that* was really hard! I've never just waited like that. And you know what? She stomped out of the kitchen and went upstairs. After about an hour or so, Julia came down smiling. 'I've cleaned my room. Go look if you don't believe me. Can I go to the dance now?' she asked sarcastically.

"You know, I wanted to shout at her, but I didn't. I simply said, 'Then you can go to the dance' — nothing else. And we didn't fight. Julia went to the dance and had a great time. When she came home, she saw the note I'd put on her pillow: 'Thank you for doing such a good job cleaning your room.'" (Catch-Them-Doing-It-Right Statement)

Children sometimes make up their minds more slowly than adults do, so many parents impatiently decide for their children. As a result, their children never learn to deal with a bad decision. Instead, parents should give children the time and the necessary facts so they can decide for themselves whenever possible.

When he was four, my son Jason wanted to have a toy motorcycle he could ride. He had seen it on television and liked it very much. The toy was expensive, and I did not want to spend the money. Telling Jason "No" would have been easy, and he would have learned nothing more than that I could say "No." Instead, I tried something else. Our discussion went something like this:

"Daddy, I want a Ride 'M Motorcycle just like on television," Jason said excitedly.

"How much money does it cost?" (Give-Me-Specific-Information Question)

"I don't know," he puzzled.

"How can you find out?" (Tell-Me-What's-On-Your-Mind Question)

"Mommy looks in the catalog," he quickly replied.

"Could we look there too?" I asked. (Give-Me-Specific-Information Question)

Jason, sad-faced, replied, "I don't know how."

"If you'll get the catalog, we can look at it together." (This-Is-The-Deal Statement)

Off he ran to get the catalog from the magazine rack.

"First," I said, "we look for 'Toys' here in the index. Now we turn to the toy section. Look, here's the Ride 'M Motorcycle. And here's the amount," I added as I pointed to the price. "It says the motorcycle costs $20." (I rounded off the $19.95 price to make things easier.)

"Do you have that much money?" I asked. (Give-Me-Specific-Information Question)

Jason's eyes lit up. "I have money in my piggy bank," he said.

After counting all the coins in his bank, now poured out on the coffee table, I said, "Jason, you have saved almost $3."

"Is that enough?" he asked.

The news was not what he hoped for. "No, you need $17 more."

I proceeded to draw a big thermometer and wrote the numbers 0 through 20 up the side.

"For every dollar you save," I said, "we can move the red mark up the thermometer one space. When the red line gets colored in to the top, you will have saved enough money."

Then I added the good news: "Here's how much you have already," pointing to the $3 mark. "You can color in the line to here now. Then, as you save each dollar, I will help you add to the line." (This-Is-The-Deal Statement — without the "if . . . then" form)

"I can do that," he declared, and began to color in the first part of the thermometer.

When he was finished, I continued our discussion: "You believe you can save the $17." (What-You-Meant Statement of intention)

"Yeah, I can do that!"

"I think you can too. (Support-Their-Thinking Statement — total support) Just remember, it will take a whole dollar to move the red line up one space. You get one dollar a week to spend."

"I want to put all of the money I save away," Jason declared enthusiastically.

"You're going to save all your money until you have enough for the Ride 'M Motorcycle." (What-You-Meant Statement of intention)

"Yeah, I'll put all my money in my bank."

Jason seemed to understand and was excited about saving the money, so I said, "We will hang up the thermometer. Then each time you put a dollar in your bank, you can color in another space. When we color in all the spaces, you will have saved enough money and we can get your Ride 'M Motorcycle." (What-You-Meant Statement of intention)

When he got his next allowance, he put the dollar into his bank. We talked about saving some for other things, but he really wanted this toy! He wound up putting all his allowances into his piggy bank until he had saved all $17. A 17-week wait for his toy was a long time for four-year-old Jason.

"There, you're finished. You did very well," I said, as Jason colored in the last of the thermometer. (Catch-Them-Doing-It-Right Statement)

Jason and I cheered enthusiastically as he jumped up and down with excitement.

"Now we have to get the Ride 'M Motorcycle. Would you like to go there this afternoon or wait until tomorrow?" (Solve-The-Problem Question)

"Let's go and get the motorcycle, Dad!"

As quickly as we could, we went out and bought his long-saved-for motorcycle. The story doesn't end there. Jason lent the motorcycle to one of his bigger friends, who broke it. Of course, Jason was upset and hoped I would buy him another one. I didn't. I decided to let him solve the problem since it was he who had let his friend ride the toy.

Because he had to save twice for the Ride 'M Motorcycle, Jason came to understand the cost of things and how long he needed to save money to buy them. Today, while he does lend some things to his friends, he is very careful about what and to whom.

Jason never forgot his first big purchase, nor did he forget the savings plan that made it possible. I could have solved this problem for him. I could also have bought the toy instead of having him save and sacrifice for it each time, but then he would not have learned its real value. Though Jason was only four, he learned to understand both the value and the time involved in reaching a goal.

Never be too quick to act for your children. Even the very young can learn important lessons when parents give them a chance.

DEALING WITH BULLIES

Schoolyard and neighborhood bullies harass many children. The parent's challenge is to help the child without taking on the bully. When possible, the harassed child should learn to deal with the bully. Here's how one parent I knew handled this problem:

Day after day, Marietta, a much bigger girl of about the same age as Rosa, chased the smaller girl on the way to her new school. Rosa would arrive with tear-filled eyes. After the first week she had had enough.

"I'm never going to school again!" Rosa cried.

"Has Marietta been bothering you again?" her mother asked. (Give-Me-Specific-Information Question)

"She never leaves me alone. She's always picking on me. I wish she were dead!" Rosa had had all she could handle. Frustration was turning to fear, and fear to real hatred of Marietta.

Her mother then supported Rosa while toning down her feelings.

"Marietta has really upset you. You're very angry at her for bullying you." (What-You-Meant Statement and Walk-In-Their-Shoes Statement)

"Every time I come home from school, she waits for me," Rosa sobbed. "Today she chased me all the way home. I'm never going to school again!"

"Marietta has you so frightened you never want to go to school again," Mother confirmed. (What-You-Meant Statement)

"I mean it, Mommy. I won't go!"

How could her mother support her and yet make Rosa realize she must still go to school? She could walk Rosa to school, but then Rosa's friends would tease her about needing her mother to baby-sit her. If her mother drove Rosa to school, they would only postpone the bullying. Calling the school would create a similar pattern. Rosa needed to learn some helpful ways to deal with this kind of problem herself.

Difficulties such as these are common among children. Unfortunately, many parents are too quick to jump in and help. They overlook the importance of letting their children learn to see the problem coming and to defend themselves, since neither parents, police, nor other people can always be there for them.

Knowing many bullies are themselves afraid and without friends, Rosa's mother found a simple solution:

"You're very upset. I would be too," Mother continued, trying to remain as calm as she could. (Walk-In-Their-Shoes Statement)

"I know I wouldn't want anyone to pick on me. I'd like to help, yet I can't always be there for you. (Support-Their-Thinking Statement — additional information) I'm sure staying home from school seems like a good idea to you. I wonder if it's the only way to solve this." (Solve-The-Problem Question)

"I won't go to school!" Rosa repeated, just as firmly as before. "I can't stop her from chasing and teasing me. She's bigger than I am."

"Marietta *is* a big girl. She must scare you. (Walk-In-Their-Shoes Statement) You think the only choice you have is to stay home," said Mother calmly. (What-You-Meant Statement)

"If I go to school, she'll just chase me again," Rosa replied, calmer but still tearful.

"You can think of nothing else," Mother said. (Think-It-Over Statement)

At this point, she sat back in her chair and waited for Rosa to think about what she had said.

After a few minutes, Rosa spoke. Her tears were all but gone now. "Well . . . you could drive me to school."

"Yes, I could drive you. (What-You-Meant Statement) What do you think the other kids would say if they saw me drive you to school every day?" (Tell-Me-What's-On-Your-Mind Question)

She could almost see the gears in Rosa's head start to move as Rosa considered the question. "They'd call me a Mama's girl."

"Rosa, you wouldn't like that either." (Walk-In-Their-Shoes Statement)

"No . . . but . . ." Her mother waited. "But . . . what else can I do? I can't think of anything."

"You can't think of *anything* to do." (Think-It-Over Statement)

Now Mother waited for what seemed to Rosa a long, long time.

Then the young girl said, "I could take the long way to school, I guess."

Mother still kept quiet, giving her daughter more time to think about it.

Finally Rosa said, "I can't think, Mommy. Can't you help me?"

Because her mother had given her a chance to get her feelings out, Rosa was now ready to consider other possibilities. Had her mother offered a solution earlier, Rosa would not have been so willing to listen.

"You know, Rosa, a big kid bullied me when I went to school. I hated it too. Like you, I got very upset. No one wants to be teased or chased. (Walk-In-Their-Shoes Statement) Your Grandma gave me an idea that worked. Maybe you could try it."

"What is it?" Rosa asked eagerly.

"Grandma told me, 'Sometimes people who want to frighten or hurt you are frightened or in some kind of pain themselves. The next time that bully goes to chase you or tease you, turn to her and stand up real tall. Then say in your loudest, firmest voice, "I want you to leave me alone!"'"

"You know, when I tried that, I couldn't believe it! It worked! Maybe it can work for you too. If you try it, I will watch from a distance to see how you do. (This-Is-The-Deal Statement) Or do you want to try it your-self?" (Solve-The-Problem Question)

"That'll never work," Rosa said. "She won't stop just because I tell her to."

"It's not worth trying." (Think-It-Over Statement)

"She's way bigger than me."

Instead of responding to Rosa's objections, she continued to urge her to try the idea: "If we practice together, then you will have the courage to try it your-self. (This-Is-The-Deal Statement) If it worked for me when I was a kid, it could work for you. Let's do it together right now before everyone gets home." (Do-It-This-Way Statement)

So practice they did. Rosa even began to laugh as her mother cowered before her daughter.

The next day, still afraid, Rosa set out, glancing back from time to time to see if Mother was still watching. She had not gone a full block before Marietta ran toward her. Rosa turned and faced her tormentor. Her words were loud and sure as she stood her ground:

"I want you to leave me alone!"

Marietta stopped in her tracks. She paused for what Rosa felt was forever. Then, going no farther, a frustrated and confused Marietta turned away, shouting, "Go on then, you baby! See if I care!"

It was as simple as that! Rosa had solved the problem.

Parents must find creative ways to help children solve their own problems, as this mother did. Children are often able to handle even tough situations if we let them. Through her unusual approach, Rosa's mother helped Rosa become a more confident, capable, and independent person.

Part 5

"Act It Out"

▶ Role-Play
What
You've
Learned

While reading Being the Parent YOU Want to Be, *have you ever . . .*

- wanted to practice the 12 communication skills before using them with your child?

- considered whether practice makes perfect with parenting too?

- wished you could work with other parents who share your concerns?

- thought, "What, me, role-play? Are you kidding!"?

This section will give you real-life practice in using the 12 Communication Skills for Effective Parenting.

INTRODUCTION

Role-playing is a tremendously effective way for small groups of parents who are reading and discussing this book to practice the 12 communication skills they have learned. There are three role-plays, or situations, in which each parent can take a part, for each of the three communications skills sections: "What Are You Thinking?" — Discovering What's On Your Child's Mind, "I Don't Want To!" — Overcoming Your Child's Objections, and "What WILL We Do?" — Solving Problems and Making Decisions With Your Child.

The role-plays work best with groups of three people each. This allows for three roles: Parent, Child, and Observer. You can also do the role-plays in pairs, having the person playing the Child also act as the Observer.

Each set of role-plays should be completed as soon as possible after reading the section it belongs to and before going on to the next one. The longer you wait to do the role-plays, the more likely you are to forget how to use the communication skills covered in that part of the book.

HOW TO ROLE-PLAY

For the first role-play case in each set, group members should decide who will play which roles. After that, rotate the roles for the other two cases in the set.

Before beginning a role-play case, read the background information for your role only. On the Role-Play Observation Sheet for each section, the Observer records the skills the *Parent* role-player uses. You will find three Role-Play Observation Sheets for each set of role-plays at the ends of Chapters 16, 17, and 18. When all role-players understand their parts, the Observer starts the role-play by asking either the Child or the Parent to begin. Begin only after you have read the communication skills for the section you intend to role-play.

Those playing the Parent should stick as much as possible to the four communication skills learned in the section they are practicing. Don't be afraid to use the more challenging communication skills in each set of four. In Part 2: "What Are You Thinking?" — Discovering What's On Your Child's Mind, for example, these are the What-You-Meant and the Think-It-Over Statements. The Parent role-player should *name each skill before using it*. This gives both you and the other members of the group a chance to correct any mistakes. For instance, the Parent role-player might say, "Think-It-Over Statement: You are having trouble with your homework." This is really a What-You-Meant Statement.

The Observer needs to make sure that the skill the Parent role-player uses is the one stated ahead of time. Observers should record the names of the communication skills Parent role-players intend to use as well as those they actually do use. (Abbreviations for the communication skills are at the bottom of each Role-Play Observation Sheet.) The record will show how often the Parent role-player uses each skill and will demonstrate how some communication skills lead naturally to others.

Those role-players taking the Child role should try to be difficult and stubborn enough to allow the Parent role-players to use the more challenging communication skills a number of times.

Allow 20 minutes for each case in a role-play session. That gives you one hour for all three cases in the set for a specific skill group.

Practicing in this way will help you learn to use the various communication skills naturally. While practice is serious business, you should approach the role-plays with a playful attitude. Have fun!

16

Role-Plays for Discovering What's On Your Child's Mind

PARENT ROLE-PLAYER INSTRUCTIONS

This role-play session will give you a chance to practice all the communication skills learned in Part 2: Tell-Me-What's-On-Your-Mind Questions, Give-Me-Specific-Information Questions, What-You-Meant Statements, and Think-It-Over Statements. Place your emphasis on the What-You-Meant and Think-It-Over Statements, which are the most challenging of the four communication skills from this section.

If you are the Parent role-player, listen carefully to the Child role-player. Then decide which skill you will use and name it out loud *before* actually using it. That way, the Observer can record it and all the group members can make sure you use the skill you have identified.

You may find your first session awkward and unnatural. This is because you can use only four communication skills, with the emphasis on just two of them. Also, stating the skill first may seem to break the flow of conversation, but it is helpful to do so. With practice, you will become increasingly comfortable using the skills.

By now, you will know that you can respond to the same Child statement in several ways. For instance, if the Child role-player were to say, "I don't know why. I just can't do this," you might answer with any of the following:

"Tell-Me-What's-On-Your-Mind Question: Why do you feel that way?"

"Give-Me-Specific-Information Question: Did you follow the instructions?"

"What-You-Meant Statement: You feel discouraged."

"Think-It-Over Statement: Deciding that you just can't do it is the best way to handle the problem."

Different parents choose different ways of replying, depending on how strict or permissive they are and on the problem itself. All of the above responses could be correct.

CHILD ROLE-PLAYER INSTRUCTIONS

If you are the Child role-player, try to think, behave, and answer as you believe the child in each case might do. Draw on your imagination and your experience.

OBSERVER INSTRUCTIONS

As the Observer, you should read *all* the Background Information for each case. It is your job to make sure the Parent role-player names the skill he or she will use *before* acting it out. On the Skill Progression Chart on the Role-Play Observation Sheets (on pages 279, 280, and 281), write down each communication skill the Parent role-player uses. You should find that most are What-You-Meant Statements and Think-It-Over Statements.

As you listen carefully to both the Parent and Child role-players, try to look for opportunities to use the What-You-Meant Statement (WYM) and the Think-It-Over Statement (TIO). If the Parent role-player misses such an opportunity, note the Child role-player's answer to the skill the Parent does use. This will be helpful to the Parent later.

At the end of the role-play, go over the Role-Play Observation Sheet with the Parent role-player. He or she may wish to clarify his or her understanding of the skills by checking back over the material in Part 2.

LET'S GET STARTED

Turn now to the background information for Case No. 1 that begins on page 276. *The Parent and Child role-players should read only the information for their roles. The Observer role-player needs to read the information for both roles.* The background information is intentionally sketchy to allow you to use your imagination and experience.

After 20 minutes, *change roles* and move on to the next role-play, Case No. 2. Do the same for Case No. 3. When everyone has had a chance to be the Parent role-player, the session ends. At that point, the Parent role-players should go over their Observation Sheets with the Observers.

CASE NO. 1

Background Information for Parent Role

You are meeting with your child after school. Earlier in the day, your child's teacher told you that your child has begun handing in homework late or sometimes not at all. Until now, the child has been turning in all assignments on time. You hope to discover why your child is falling behind and find a solution to any problem he or she might have. Your child has an after-school job.

Background Information for Child Role

Your parent wants to speak to you after you come home from school. You think you know why. Earlier your teacher had talked to you about handing in your homework late. Until now, you have been turning in all assignments on time and have done well in school. You recently took an after-school job to earn some money to buy something you have wanted for a long time. This has left you with less time for studying. What's more, now you don't have much time to hang out with your friends.

As you begin to role-play, act anxious, perhaps even defensive. Then, as you go along, open up more.

CASE NO. 2

Background Information for Parent Role

Your family has recently moved to a new city. It is not like your previous home, and your child hasn't made new friends. The child is unhappy and withdrawn, even at home. You want to help your child. You want to get your child to talk about it and make him or her feel comfortable in the new city.

Background Information for Child Role

Your family has recently moved to a new city. It isn't like your previous home, where you had many friends. Here you've made no new friends. Unfortunately, this new city is strange and uncomfortable for you. You think the kids don't like you and don't want to be friends because you are new. This has made you unhappy, and you have withdrawn from everyone, even at home.

You want to get over this problem, but don't know how or why you feel as you do. You have just arrived home with your brother or sister. Your parent has asked to speak to you privately in your room. At first you are afraid that you have done something wrong.

CASE NO. 3

Background Information for Parent Role
One of your children has come stomping into the house after losing a baseball game. The child seems frustrated and angry. Your child is at least an average baseball player. Unfortunately, your child wants to win all the time in everything he or she does. You feel the child may be setting standards that are too high, but you don't know why. While the rest of the family is doing something else, you sit down with your child and begin to talk casually about baseball.

Background Information for Child Role
You are a bright young child who needs to win all the time. Your coach and your parent have cheered you on. The team you play for has just lost an important game because you made an error. As a result, you stomp through the door, upset and angry. Most of the family is busy. Your parent comes into your room to talk about the game that has upset you.

Role-Play Observation Sheet for Discovering What's On Your Child's Mind

Case No. 1 — Parent role-player: _____

Remember to end the role-play after 20 minutes.

Skill Progression Chart

1. _____	11. _____	21. _____
2. _____	12. _____	22. _____
3. _____	13. _____	23. _____
4. _____	14. _____	24. _____
5. _____	15. _____	25. _____
6. _____	16. _____	26. _____
7. _____	17. _____	27. _____
8. _____	18. _____	28. _____
9. _____	19. _____	29. _____
10. _____	20. _____	30. _____

Abbreviations:

Tell-Me-What's-On-Your-Mind Question (TWM)

Give-Me-Specific-Information Question (GSI)

What-You-Meant Statement (WYM)

Think-It-Over Statement (TIO)

Comments:

Role-Play Observation Sheet for Discovering What's On Your Child's Mind

Case No. 2 — Parent role-player: _____

Remember to end the role-play after 20 minutes.

Skill Progression Chart

1. _____	11. _____	21. _____
2. _____	12. _____	22. _____
3. _____	13. _____	23. _____
4. _____	14. _____	24. _____
5. _____	15. _____	25. _____
6. _____	16. _____	26. _____
7. _____	17. _____	27. _____
8. _____	18. _____	28. _____
9. _____	19. _____	29. _____
10. _____	20. _____	30. _____

Abbreviations:

Tell-Me-What's-On-Your-Mind Question (TWM)

Give-Me-Specific-Information Question (GSI)

What-You-Meant Statement (WYM)

Think-It-Over Statement (TIO)

Comments:

Role-Play Observation Sheet for Discovering What's On Your Child's Mind

Case No. 3 — Parent role-player: _____

Remember to end the role-play after 20 minutes.

Skill Progression Chart

1. _____	11. _____	21. _____
2. _____	12. _____	22. _____
3. _____	13. _____	23. _____
4. _____	14. _____	24. _____
5. _____	15. _____	25. _____
6. _____	16. _____	26. _____
7. _____	17. _____	27. _____
8. _____	18. _____	28. _____
9. _____	19. _____	29. _____
10. _____	20. _____	30. _____

Abbreviations:

Tell-Me-What's-On-Your-Mind Question (TWM)

Give-Me-Specific-Information Question (GSI)

What-You-Meant Statement (WYM)

Think-It-Over Statement (TIO)

Comments:

17

Role-Plays for Overcoming Your Child's Objections

*T*his role-playing session gives you a chance to practice the communication skills learned so far. This time you will concentrate on the Overcoming Objections skills: Look-On-The-Bright-Side Statements (LOBS), Walk-In-Their-Shoes Statements (WITS), Support-Their-Thinking Statements (STT), and Catch-Them-Doing-It-Right Statements (CTDR). As before, use your experience and imagination to create your role convincingly.

Be sure to look for the positive qualities in the child. Back up the child's feelings with Walk-In-Their-Shoes Statements and the child's ideas with Support-Their-Thinking Statements. Recognize the child's sense of pride with Catch-Them-Doing-It-Right Statements.

Again, be sure to name the skill you decide to use *before* you say it. Keep in mind that the child may tell you one thing, while his or her tone of voice and body language may show another thing, such as hurt feelings or wounded pride. Parent role-players read the Background Information on page 284,

Child role-players read instructions at the bottom of this page and Observers read page 285.

PARENT ROLE-PLAYER INSTRUCTIONS

Practice using the communication skills of Part 3: Walk-In-Their-Shoes Statements, Support-Their-Thinking Statements, Catch-Them-Doing-It-Right Statements, and Look-On-The-Bright-Side Statements. As you read the background information for each case, look for opportunities to use the more challenging communication skills in this section: Walk-In-Their-Shoes Statements (challenging because you have to express real empathy rather than sympathy) and Catch-Them-Doing-It-Right Statements (challenging because you must give approval for actions the child values instead of giving praise for accomplishments). Listen carefully to the Child role-player's answers and watch his or her body language. Be alert to your own feelings and body language. While we want your communication skills to fit your parenting style, you will gain benefit from trying communication skills that may not come easily to you. Try them — you may like them and the results they get!

Again, *remember to name each skill you intend to use before you use it.*

CHILD ROLE-PLAYER INSTRUCTIONS

You are going to help the Parent role-player practice using the Overcoming Your Child's Objections skills of Part 3: Walk-In-Their-Shoes Statements (WITS), Support-Their-Thinking Statements (STT), Catch-Them-Doing-It-Right Statements (CTDR), and Look-On-The-Bright-Side Statements (LOBS).

Try to think, behave, and act like a child. Use your imagination. You might try being hostile, sullen, defensive, or indifferent. Be challenging enough to inspire the Parent role-player to use the communication skills learned so far, especially the more challenging Walk-In-Their-Shoes and Catch-Them-Doing-It-Right Statements. If the Parent role-player makes good use of the communication skills for overcoming objections, you may find a change in your attitude. Let yourself go.

OBSERVER INSTRUCTIONS

As the Observer, read all the Background Information for each case. *Make sure the Parent role-player names the skill he or she will use before acting it out.* On the Role-Play Observation Sheets (pages 290, 291, and 292), record the communication skill the Parent role-player uses.

Listen for opportunities to use the Walk-In-Their-Shoes Statements (WITS) and Catch-Them-Doing-It-Right Statements (CTDR). If the Parent role-player misses such an opportunity, note the Child role-player's answer to the skill the Parent *does* use. This will be helpful to the Parent later.

At the end of the role-play, go over the Role-Play Observation Sheet with the Parent role-player. He or she may wish to review the material about these four skills in Part 3.

CASE NO. 1

Background Information for Parent Role

Your child is a high school senior with whom you have a good relationship. Your child has been depressed for several days since receiving a rejection from the college he or she wanted to attend.

This is a persistent teen who has achieved high grades through hard work. Along the way, he or she gave up all extracurricular activities in order to study harder. Not taking part in these activities may be why the college rejected your child's application.

You know your child wants to be a doctor, just like a favorite uncle. You know that not getting into the desired college will affect this goal. You also know that the goal of becoming a doctor may have been unrealistic. You recognize that competition with other premed students may make it impossible for your child to get into the medical field at all.

Right now you are chatting with your child in the living room. You are talking about how disappointed he or she is. You want to suggest that the child might consider a related career. Tell the child he or she could take the aptitude testing available at the high school to help set a new goal.

Background Information for Child Role

Try to use language and behavior that will encourage your Parent role-player to use the communication skills we have learned in this section: Look-On-The-Bright-Side Statements (LOBS), Catch Them Doing It Right Statements (CTDR), Support-Their-Thinking Statements (STT), Walk-In-Their-Shoes Statements (WITS). Noted in parentheses are skills the Parent role-player could use when responding to you, depending on how you present the situation.

You are a high school senior who was told a few days ago that you were rejected by the college or university you wanted to attend. This has really upset you. (WITS)

You have decided to become a doctor, like a favorite uncle. You have spent every waking moment trying to make this happen. Because studying doesn't come easily to you (WITS), you have worked hard. You have even given up most of your outside activities to gain more time for study. Getting high grades has been a struggle. (CTDR, STT, WITS)

You wanted to become a doctor because your uncle, a prominent physician, encouraged you to enter the medical field. (STT) Maybe because he doesn't have children of his own, this uncle treats you like his own child. (WITS) He is excited that you want to be a doctor too. In fact, he has given you money to help pay your medical school tuition. (STT)

You are sitting in the living room, talking to your parent. Until now, you have convinced yourself that medicine is the only career for you (STT), but you are beginning to have your doubts. Gradually tell your parent about your worries. Slowly realize that you may have chosen this career because of your uncle's encouragement, and because you don't really know what else you want to do. Perhaps you were swept up by his excitement and the money for medical school, rather than by your own desire to become a doctor.

CASE NO. 2

Background Information for Parent Role

A neighbor has just called to tell you that his or her child and yours were "playing doctor" between the garages. Your neighbor was angry, and now you are upset. You know that playing doctor *may* be normal for children of this age, but you are still concerned. Like many parents, you have trouble accepting this action as normal, and you want to make sure your child doesn't repeat it in the future.

Begin by asking your child to tell his or her side of the story. You want to be reasonable for your child's sake, yet you realize that his or her activity could create future problems.

Background Information for Child Role

Noted in parentheses are skills the Parent role-player could use when responding to you, depending on how you present the situation.

You are a young child of about seven. You are just arriving home after a neighbor found you and his or her child "playing doctor." The neighbor was upset and even called you a "dirty little animal." (STT, WITS, LOBS) You are hurt and puzzled by the neighbor's anger. (WITS) You enjoyed the game, but also sensed that you were doing something wrong. (STT with additional information) Fortunately, your parent doesn't seem upset, but because of your own feelings and the neighbor's harsh words, you are still worried about what your parent will do.

CASE NO. 3

Background Information for Parent Role

You walk into your child's room to talk about a fight that took place earlier that day. Your child pushed a friend to the ground, thinking that the friend was making fun of him or her. Your child wouldn't listen to your explanation that the friend was only trying to be funny.

Your child is often aggressive and frequently overreacts. This creates frequent minor upsets at home and in the neighborhood. As a result, your child has few friends. While talking with the child, look for the good parts of his or her personality. Help your child recognize the difference between bad-mouthing and friendly teasing. You also want your child to learn to be less hotheaded.

Background Information for Child Role

Noted in parentheses are skills the Parent role-player could use when responding to you, depending on how you present the situation.

Earlier today you got into a fight with your friend. The friend said something that seemed like an insult, so you angrily pushed your friend to the ground. (WYM) You get mad easily (WYM, WITS) and are not inclined to let anyone get away with offending you. Often your overreactions cause problems at home and in your neighborhood. (TIO)

You admire your parent, who has taught you always to stand up for your rights. (CTDR, STT) Now you respond to your parent by defending yourself. (WITS, STT with additional information) As your parent shows that he or she understands and supports you, you gradually begin to realize that there is a difference between an insult and friendly teasing.

Role-Play Observation Sheet for Overcoming Your Child's Objections

Case No. 1 — Parent role-player: _____

Remember to end the role-play after 20 minutes.

Skill Progression Chart

1. _____	11. _____	21. _____
2. _____	12. _____	22. _____
3. _____	13. _____	23. _____
4. _____	14. _____	24. _____
5. _____	15. _____	25. _____
6. _____	16. _____	26. _____
7. _____	17. _____	27. _____
8. _____	18. _____	28. _____
9. _____	19. _____	29. _____
10. _____	20. _____	30. _____

Abbreviations:

Tell-Me-What's-On-Your-Mind Question (TWM)

Give-Me-Specific-Information Question (GSI)

What-You-Meant Statement (WYM)

Think-It-Over Statement (TIO)

Look-On-The-Bright-Side Statement (LOBS)

Walk-In-Their-Shoes Statement (WITS)

Support-Their-Thinking Statement (STT)

Catch-Them-Doing-It-Right Statement (CTDR)

Comments:

Role-Play Observation Sheet for
Overcoming Your Child's Objections

Case No. 2 — Parent role-player: _____

Remember to end the role-play after 20 minutes.

Skill Progression Chart

1. _____	11. _____	21. _____
2. _____	12. _____	22. _____
3. _____	13. _____	23. _____
4. _____	14. _____	24. _____
5. _____	15. _____	25. _____
6. _____	16. _____	26. _____
7. _____	17. _____	27. _____
8. _____	18. _____	28. _____
9. _____	19. _____	29. _____
10. _____	20. _____	30. _____

Abbreviations:

Tell-Me-What's-On-Your-Mind Question (TWM)

Give-Me-Specific-Information Question (GSI)

What-You-Meant Statement (WYM)

Think-It-Over Statement (TIO)

Look-On-The-Bright-Side Statement (LOBS)

Walk-In-Their-Shoes Statement (WITS)

Support-Their-Thinking Statement (STT)

Catch-Them-Doing-It-Right Statement (CTDR)

Comments:

Role-Play Observation Sheet for Overcoming Your Child's Objections

Case No. 3 — Parent role-player: _____

Remember to end the role-play after 20 minutes.

Skill Progression Chart

1. _____	11. _____	21. _____
2. _____	12. _____	22. _____
3. _____	13. _____	23. _____
4. _____	14. _____	24. _____
5. _____	15. _____	25. _____
6. _____	16. _____	26. _____
7. _____	17. _____	27. _____
8. _____	18. _____	28. _____
9. _____	19. _____	29. _____
10. _____	20. _____	30. _____

Abbreviations:

Tell-Me-What's-On-Your-Mind Question (TWM)

Give-Me-Specific-Information Question (GSI)

What-You-Meant Statement (WYM)

Think-It-Over Statement (TIO)

Look-On-The-Bright-Side Statement (LOBS)

Walk-In-Their-Shoes Statement (WITS)

Support-Their-Thinking Statement (STT)

Catch-Them-Doing-It-Right Statement (CTDR)

Comments:

18

Role-Plays for Solving Problems and Making Decisions With Your Child

*T*he emphasis in this section is on Solve-The-Problem and Decision-Making communication skills. While you may need Out-Of-Bounds or Do-It-This-Way Statements occasionally, use the various forms of the Solve-The-Problem Question and This-Is-The-Deal Statement more often, as these are the more challenging communication skills. This-Is-The-Deal Statements can prove a challenge because you have to trust the child to do his or her part. The Out-Of-Bounds Statement can also be challenging because it must be stated in positive rather than negative terms.

As before, *the Parent role-player will name each skill before using it.* Parent role-players, Child role-players, and Observers read your instructions on page 294.

PARENT ROLE-PLAYER INSTRUCTIONS

Before you begin, and while you are role-playing, try to think about the mix of communication skills you will use. Your thinking might go like this:

> It seems in this role-play the child has a personal problem. I think I'll try to identify the problem by asking Tell-Me-What's-On-Your-Mind Questions. Some What-You-Meant Statements might be good too. I like the This-Is-The-Deal Statement rather than the Solve-The-Problem Question here, because this child may respond well to making a deal.

CHILD ROLE-PLAYER INSTRUCTIONS

This role-play session will stress resolving problems. First, mentally define what kind of character you will play. You should be difficult, yet not impossible, encouraging the Parent role-player to practice the Solve-The-Problem Question and the This-Is-The-Deal Statement. Noted in parentheses are skills the Parent role-player could use when responding to you, depending on how you present the situation.

OBSERVER INSTRUCTIONS

Read the Background Information for the Parent and Child roles for each case. In this session, the Parent role-player will decide on the communication-skill mix to use before using it. Then, as before, he or she will name the skill first, then state it. If the Parent forgets, ask to have the communication skill identified.

Note the communication skills that produce a positive change in the Child. As before, note where the Parent role-player might have used another skill effectively.

On the Skill Progression Charts, record the name of each skill as the Parent role-player uses it. Try to find good opportunities for the Parent to use the more challenging Solve-The-Problem Questions (STP) and This-Is-The-Deal Statements (TTD). If the Parent role-player misses such opportunities, note how the Child role-player responds to the skill that *is* used. This will be helpful to the Parent later. Again, at the end of the role-play, tell the Parent role-player what you found.

Noted in parentheses in the Background Information for the Child role are skills the Parent role-player could use when responding to the Child, depending on how the Child role-player presents the situation.

CASE NO. 1

Background Information for Parent Role

With the help of the guidance department, you arranged for your child to transfer this year to a new school. You arranged this with the guidance department of the old school because your child started hanging out with a bad crowd. The child also had some minor run-ins with the police. Everyone, except your child, believed the change was necessary to separate your child from the bad crowd.

Records show that your child did well in the old school until the middle of last term, when friends began to have a negative influence. Your child had been doing especially well in writing, and had even edited the school newspaper.

Since transferring, your child has made no new friends, nor has schoolwork improved. In addition, the child is belligerent and hostile toward both schoolmates and you.

Today your child angrily refused to run an errand for you. You see this as another sign of hostility and are about to have a talk with your child. What-You-Meant Statements, Think-It-Over Statements, and Support-Their-Thinking Statements (adding additional information) may be useful to start the discussion.

Background Information for Child Role

You were recently moved to a new school because your parents and the counselor at your old school wanted to get you away from the bad influence of new friends, members of a gang called the Downstreet Devils. The police had been questioning you about destroying property and stealing. Though you hadn't been a part of it, you did know who was. You had even sold a stolen bike to a friend.

Before you joined the gang, you had done well in school, even acting as editor of the school newspaper. (CTDR) Now you are angry and upset because of the move. (WITS) You refuse to make friends at the new school and you won't cooperate with your parents. (OB) You are angry and argue with everyone. Today you refused to run an errand for your parent. (TTD) You're sure your parent is going to be angry, so you're ready for a fight. Gradually, though, you begin to let go of your anger and listen to your Parent role-player. (STP)

While this gradual willingness to listen and get along may not always happen in real life, it is useful in our role-playing practice because it shows how the different communication skills work, and shows how particular skills lead to certain responses.

CASE NO. 2

Background Information for Parent Role

You are the parent of a bright eleven-year-old. Lately your child has become touchy and resents any instructions you give. Today your child surprised you with an especially strong temper tantrum after you asked that a dinner plate left standing in the drying rack be rewashed and dried. The child rewashed it, but with a great deal of slamming and banging. Since you have always had a rule that dishes must be cleaned and dried properly, your child's angry response suggests that he or she has some deeper problems.

Background Information for Child Role

You are a bright eleven-year-old who studies hard and does well in sports. (CTDR) But you are upset that your parent always insists on perfection and constantly points out your sister's accomplishments. (WYM) Your parent always criticizes you whenever anything is not just so, putting you down and frequently asking, "Why can't you be like your sister?" You hate this. (WYM, WITS, TTD)

Increasingly, you hit the roof when this happens. (STP, OB) Today you threw an especially strong temper tantrum after your parent asked you to rewash a dinner plate left standing in the drying rack. To you, it seems like just one more attempt to humiliate you. (WITS, STT, STP, TTD)

CASE NO. 3

Background Information for Parent Role

You are the parent of a high school student who recently turned eighteen. The child had been a good student, but now that he or she has become a legal adult, your child has decided not to obey other people's rules. Your teenager now skips school, smokes, and neglects his or her schoolwork.

The most recent incident occurred today, when your child came home smelling of alcohol. After giving him or her a cooling-off period, you have come to your teenager's room to talk.

Background Information for Child Role

You are a high school senior who has just turned eighteen. Until now, you have been an "obedient child": you have done well in school and cooperated with your parents at home. (CTDR) You certainly didn't dream of challenging anybody. Now that you are an adult, you have decided you don't have to follow anybody else's rules. (STP, TTD, OB, DITW) You now cut school, smoke, and neglect your studies. Today you came home after school with alcohol on your breath and your parent could smell it. (OB, DITW, TWM)

After giving you time to think about it, your parent has just walked into your room.

Role-Play Observation Sheet for Solving Problems and Making Decisions With Your Child

Case No. 1 — Parent role-player: _____

Remember to end the role-play after 20 minutes.

Skill Progression Chart

1. _____	11. _____	21. _____
2. _____	12. _____	22. _____
3. _____	13. _____	23. _____
4. _____	14. _____	24. _____
5. _____	15. _____	25. _____
6. _____	16. _____	26. _____
7. _____	17. _____	27. _____
8. _____	18. _____	28. _____
9. _____	19. _____	29. _____
10. _____	20. _____	30. _____

Abbreviations:

Tell-Me-What's-On-Your-Mind Question (TWM)
Give-Me-Specific-Information Question (GSI)
What-You-Meant Statement (WYM)
Think-It-Over Statement (TIO)
Look-On-The-Bright-Side Statement (LOBS)
Walk-In-Their-Shoes Statement (WITS)
Support-Their-Thinking Statement (STT)
Catch-Them-Doing-It-Right Statement (CTDR)
Solve-The-Problem Question (STP)
This-Is-The-Deal Statement (TTD)
Out-Of-Bounds Statement (OB)
Do-It-This-Way Statement (DITW)

Comments:

Role-Play Observation Sheet for Solving Problems and Making Decisions With Your Child

Case No. 2 — Parent role-player: _____

Remember to end the role-play after 20 minutes.

Skill Progression Chart

1. _____	11. _____	21. _____
2. _____	12. _____	22. _____
3. _____	13. _____	23. _____
4. _____	14. _____	24. _____
5. _____	15. _____	25. _____
6. _____	16. _____	26. _____
7. _____	17. _____	27. _____
8. _____	18. _____	28. _____
9. _____	19. _____	29. _____
10. _____	20. _____	30. _____

Abbreviations:
Tell-Me-What's-On-Your-Mind Question (TWM)
Give-Me-Specific-Information Question (GSI)
What-You-Meant Statement (WYM)
Think-It-Over Statement (TIO)
Look-On-The-Bright-Side Statement (LOBS)
Walk-In-Their-Shoes Statement (WITS)
Support-Their-Thinking Statement (STT)
Catch-Them-Doing-It-Right Statement (CTDR)
Solve-The-Problem Question (STP)
This-Is-The-Deal Statement (TTD)
Out-Of-Bounds Statement (OB)
Do-It-This-Way Statement (DITW)

Comments:

Role-Play Observation Sheet for Solving Problems and Making Decisions With Your Child

Case No. 3 — Parent role-player: _____

Remember to end the role-play after 20 minutes.

Skill Progression Chart

1. _____	11. _____	21. _____
2. _____	12. _____	22. _____
3. _____	13. _____	23. _____
4. _____	14. _____	24. _____
5. _____	15. _____	25. _____
6. _____	16. _____	26. _____
7. _____	17. _____	27. _____
8. _____	18. _____	28. _____
9. _____	19. _____	29. _____
10. _____	20. _____	30. _____

Abbreviations:

Tell-Me-What's-On-Your-Mind Question (TWM)

Give-Me-Specific-Information Question (GSI)

What-You-Meant Statement (WYM)

Think-It-Over Statement (TIO)

Look-On-The-Bright-Side Statement (LOBS)

Walk-In-Their-Shoes Statement (WITS)

Support-Their-Thinking Statement (STT)

Catch-Them-Doing-It-Right Statement (CTDR)

Solve-The-Problem Question (STP)

This-Is-The-Deal Statement (TTD)

Out-Of-Bounds Statement (OB)

Do-It-This-Way Statement (DITW)

Comments:

CONCLUSION

You have now completed the role-play practice for each communication skill section. You might want to go on and role-play using *all* the communication skills of *Being the Parent YOU Want to Be*. If so, go back and use all the communication skills from the earlier sessions with the case studies provided. Remember to name the communication skills before you use them.

On the other hand, you might create some role-play situations of your own. The members of every group have experiences with their own children they can draw on. Use these to construct new role-playing opportunities.

Part 6

Put It All Together

▶ Now
You Have
12
Communication
Skills

Would you like to know . . .

- how you have done?

- what style of parenting you use now that you have new skills?

- whether you've really got it right?

- how another parent has put all the skills together?

This section will show you how well you've done.

19

What Is My Parenting Style NOW?

*Y*ou have now come full circle. You began this book by discovering whether your *preferred* parenting style and your *actual* style were similar. Then you learned three groups of skills, each including four specific communication skills. The first group uncovered what your children were thinking. The second group overcame their objections. The last group focused on problem solving and decision making. Appendix A summarizes these 12 communication skills for you.

The exercises you completed have given you a good understanding of *how* and *when* to use the *12 Communication Skills for Effective Parenting*. Each can help you be the parent you want to be. Take a moment now and look at the exercises and charts you completed in Chapter 1. Also look at Table 1: Range of Decision Making on page 316. This table, and the various practices and worksheets you completed, will help you decide how you want to parent in the future. First they helped you discover your current parenting style. Then they helped you master the communication skills that will take you to where you want to go. Now they will show you how to get there.

Of course, not all parents want to change. Some are happy where they are. Others may be shocked to see how different their actual parenting styles are from the styles they thought they were using. Some of these parents want to move toward their preferred parenting styles. Others would like to improve by using the communication skills with their present approach. Once you know which group you fall into, the next step is easy — simply use those communication skills that achieve your goals.

CONGRUENCY CHECKUP

When you talk to your children about their problems, observe what communication skills you are using. You will note that you use some skills more than others. We have provided Worksheet 6: Congruency Checkup for you on page 312 to record your observations. During a week's period, use this worksheet to keep a list of how many times you use each type of communication skill.

You will notice on the worksheet that in the first column across from each skill are lines. You can use hash marks (////) on these lines to record the number of times you use each skill. For example, ten hash marks means you used that particular skill ten times during the observation week. (So that you understand better how to fill out this worksheet, we have given you a sample on page 336, in Appendix I.)

The next three columns across from the skills show whether a skill is a My Way, Our Way, or Your Way parenting style. These columns have lines for you to convert the hash marks to percentages of use for each communication skill.

The easiest way to use this worksheet is to make a total of 100 observations for the week. In this way, the *total number of times* you use a particular communication skill would also equal the *percentage* for that skill. For example, if you made 100 observations during the week and used Tell-Me-What's-On-Your-Mind Questions six times, that equals 6 percent. Or, if you used What-You-Meant Statements four times, that equals 4 percent. The same holds true for all other communication skills used during a 100-observation week.

If you make less than 100 observations, you would divide the number of times you used a particular skill (S) by the total number of observations (O) you made. Then you would multiply your answer by 100. For example:

$$\text{S} \quad \div \quad \text{O} \quad \text{X} \quad 100 = \text{percentage}$$

number of   total
times a skill   observations
was used

Suppose you made a total of 50 observations and used What-You-Meant Statements three times. To determine the percentage use of that particular skill, you would do the following math:

$$3 \quad \div \quad 50 \quad = .06 \text{ X } 100 = 6\%$$

What-You-   total
Meant   observations
Statements

Therefore, during your 50 observations you used What-You-Meant Statements 6 percent of the time.

When you have completed your observation week and recorded all of the percentages for each skill, you can discover which parenting style you now use most by adding up the percentage columns. For example, if the My Way column shows that you used Give-Me-Specific-Information Questions 11 percent of the time, Hobson's Choice 1 percent of the time, and Do-It-This-Way Statements 11 percent of the time, your total for using My Way skills is 23 percent.

Please use Worksheet 6 below to record each of your observations and percentages.

Worksheet 6
Congruency Checkup

	No. of Observations	MW	Percentages OW	YW
Skills for Discovering What's On Your Child's Mind				
Tell-Me-What's-On-Your-Mind Question				
Give-Me-Specific-Information Question				
What-You-Meant Statement				
Think-It-Over Statement				
Skills for Overcoming Your Child's Objections				
Look-On-The-Bright-Side Statement				
Walk-In-Their-Shoes Statement				
Pointed to success				
Another direction				
Support-Their-Thinking Statement				
Total support				
Gave additional information				
Catch-Them-Doing-It-Right Statement				
Skills for Solving Problems and Making Decisions With Your Child				
Solve-The-Problem Question				
Asked for solutions:				
broad solutions				
narrow solutions				
very narrow solutions				
Offered choices:				
equal choices				
limited choices				
Hobson's Choice				
This-Is-The-Deal Statement				
Parent acts first				
Child acts first				
Out-Of-Bounds Statement				
Do-It-this-Way Statement				
Totals: MW + OW + YW = 100%				

ARE YOU STILL CONGRUENT?

Look at the results of Worksheet 6. This will help you see what your actual parenting style is at this point. The totals of each column show how often you kept, shared, or gave away decision-making control. If you always let your children decide, you will have used only the communication skills in column YW (Your Way — Permissive — Child's Decision). If you decided everything yourself, you will have used only the communication skills in column MW (My Way — Authoritarian — Parent's Decision).

Most parents fall somewhere between these two extremes. You will probably use some communication skills in the OW column (Our Way — Authoritative — Shared Decision), unless your children are either quite young or very mature. The younger your children, the more you must decide for them. As they grow up, you will probably want to let them make more of their own decisions. Yet, even if you have grown teenagers, they probably won't make *all* of the decisions that affect them while they live with you.

Parents will always struggle to find the best approach. No parent succeeds 100 percent of the time. When we do fail, we must learn to forgive ourselves, accept our mistakes, and move on.

Compare your actual parenting style with the style you want to achieve. The closer the two match, the more in agreement — or congruent — these two styles will be. The more congruent and consistent you are, the freer your children will be to learn and grow. Keeping your actual parenting style and your desired style in agreement is a matter of following either, or both, of these steps:

1. Use more communication skills from the parenting style you favor.

2. Use fewer communication skills from the parenting style you want to avoid.

It is that simple!

COMMUNICATION SKILLS AND PARENTING STYLES CHART

Now look at the following Table 1: Range of Decision Making on page 316. Here you will find the *12 Communication Skills for Effective Parenting* arranged to show whether a skill is:

Authoritarian (My Way)
Authoritative (Our Way)
Permissive (Your Way)

You will probably use each skill at some time. This is true no matter what parenting style you use most of the time.

If you want to *share* more decision-making control, use more of these communication skills:

Tell-Me-What's-On-Your-Mind Questions (TWM)
What-You-Meant Statements (WYM)
Look-On-The-Bright-Side Statements (LOBS)
Walk-In-Their-Shoes Statements (WITS — pointing to other successes)
Support-Their-Thinking Statements (STT — giving total support)
Catch-Them-Doing-It-Right Statements (CTDR)
This-Is-The-Deal Statements (TTD — loose parent control, parent acts first)
Solve-The-Problem Questions (STP — equal choices or allow a broad range of possible solutions)

If you want to *keep* more control of decision making for yourself, use these communication skills:

Give-Me-Specific-Information Questions (GSI)
Think-It-Over Statements (TIO)
Support-Their-Thinking Statements (STT — giving additional information)
This-Is-The-Deal Statements (TTD — tight parent control, child acts first)
Solve-The-Problem Questions (STP — Hobson's Choice or allow for a narrow or very narrow range of possible solutions)
Out-Of-Bounds Statements (OB — directed at acts, not at children themselves)
Do-It-This-Way Statements (DITW)
Look-On-The-Bright-Side Statements (LOBS)

If you want to *give* more control of decision making to your children, use these communication skills:

Tell-Me-What's-On-Your-Mind Questions (TWM)
Look-On-The-Bright-Side Statements (LOBS)
Support-Their-Thinking Statements (STT — giving total support)
Catch-Them-Doing-It-Right Statements (CTDR)
Solve-The-Problem Questions (STP — equal choices or allow a broad range of possible solutions)
What-You-Meant Statements (WYM)
This-Is-The-Deal Statements (TTD — loose parent control, parent acts first)

Table 1
Range of Decision Making

Parent Decision   **Child Decision**

100%	90%	80%	70%	60%	50%	60%	70%	80%	90%	100%
Skills for Discovering What's On Your Child's Mind										
GSI				TIO			WYM			TWM
Skills for Overcoming Your Child's Objections										
LOBS					LOBS					LOBS
							WITS			
STT (with additional information)					STT (with additional information)					STT (total support)
CTDR					CTDR					CTDR
Skills for Solving Problems and Making Decisions With Your Child										
		STP (very narrow solutions)			STP (narrow solutions)					STP (broad solutions)
STP unequal choices, Hobson's Choice					STP (limited equal choices)					STP (equal choices)
		TTD (tight parent control - child acts first)						TTD (loose parent control - parent acts first)		
OB										
DITW										

My Way   **Our Way**   **Your Way**

THEY DID IT, SO CAN YOU: CALIFORNIA BOUND!

Few family adventures let parents use the range of *12 Communication Skills for Effective Parenting* in the way the following story does. Several years ago, when their two youngest children were still in elementary school and the two oldest in high school, our closest friends took the family trip of a lifetime.

Our story begins at dinner, early one fall evening in Canada. The family's relatives in California were the center-piece of part of the trip — the rest of the trip was a potpourri of each family member's interests.

> "We've decided to go visit Uncle Dan and Aunt Elly in Los Angeles next summer," Ronnie, the father, announced. "You'll get lots of time with your cousins Aaron and Sarah."

Carol, the mother, held up a large, mounted map of the southern part of Canada and the entire United States. She then stuck two large red-topped pins into the map — one in Toronto and one in Los Angeles.

> "We plan to follow roughly this route," Ronnie added, as he traced the route on the map with his finger. "We will be gone for two months."

> "That's great!" shouted Deborah Beth.

> "Can I help get ready?" Stephen chimed in.

> "We can all help," Michelle added.

> "What can I do?" Andrew wanted to know.

"If we're going to have fun and not drive each other crazy, we'll have to work together," Carol said. (Support-Their-Thinking Statement)

To that Ronnie added, "And that means all of us. (Giving additional information to the Support-Their-Thinking Statement) Now then, we'll need to get details about all the places we'll pass through. Your mother has suggested we use envelopes for each state and put all the information we gather in them. How many will we need, then?" (Give-Me-Specific-Information Question)

The children counted each state as their eyes followed the black line their father had drawn on the map. "Sixteen!" Andrew shouted out. Being the oldest, he could trace the route more quickly.

"Right on! You're fast," his mother said. (Catch-Them-Doing-It-Right Statement) "And here is where we'll put everything we get." (Do-It-This-Way Statement)

Carol, who is the most creative teacher I have ever known, was well prepared. She had already mounted 16 envelopes on a separate board. "Now we need to decide who will do what. (What-You-Meant Statement — referring back to each child's desire to be involved) First we have to figure out what we will need if we are going to have a trip we will all enjoy. (Look-On-The-Bright-Side Statement) What are some of those things?" (Tell-Me-What's-On-Your-Mind Question)

"We'll need to know what places there are to visit," Andrew began.

"And we want to know where we can do some shopping," Michelle added.

"I want to go to Disneyland!" shouted Deborah Beth.

"Me too!" Stephen proclaimed. The older children nodded in agreement.

Already everyone was getting excited about the trip.

"Okay! We're definitely going to Disneyland," Ronnie confirmed. (Support-Their-Thinking Statement — total agreement) "Dan and Elly have already said they're going to take us when we get there."

"Awesome!" the others cried.

"Where can we get the information we need?" Carol asked. (Tell-Me-What's-On-Your-Mind Question)

"Encyclopedias."

"The library."

"We can ask a travel agency!"

"On the Internet."

"Don't forget the Chamber of Commerce."

One after the other, Stephen, Deborah Beth, Michelle, and Andrew answered their mother. Their enthusiasm was growing by the moment.

"Oh!" Michelle exclaimed as she jumped up from her seat. "And we can check in the old *National Geographics* we have too."

"That's an excellent idea," Ronnie said. (Catch-Them-Doing-It-Right Statement) "I think we could save some time if we started with the travel agency, so we will do that. (Do-It-This-Way Statement) They can help us plan the best route for what we want to do. Do we want to get to Los Angeles quickly, or do we want to see a lot of things on the way? What do you think? (Tell-Me-What's-On-Your-Mind Question) We've got two months, so we can take our time."

"How long are we going to be staying in California?" asked Andrew.

"We plan to stay with Dan and Elly for about two weeks," replied Carol. "Then we'll start back. If we come back a different way, we can see and do more things along the way."

"That's great!" Michelle declared excitedly. "I'd like to see Yellowstone National Park."

"I want to go to Tombstone," said Stephen. "And I want to see the sorrel cactus!"

Finally Deborah Beth added her two cents' worth: "I want to see the Grand Canyon. I saw it on television and it's awesome."

"They're all great ideas," Carol assured them. (Catch-Them-Doing-It-Right Statement) "Hopefully, we'll all get to do and see many things."

"We won't be able to do everything, but we can all do something we want," Ronnie said.

Over the next few weeks, the family made several trips to the travel agency. Sometimes they all went together, and sometimes Ronnie or Carol went with one or more of the children. Before long, a gold mine of travel brochures, schedules, and maps accumulated in the family room.

While they were gathering this material, the older children, Michelle and Andrew, scanned the encyclopedias and looked up things on the Internet, and Ronnie and Carol provided additional research from other sources. All the younger children went through the *National Geographic* magazines the family had collected over many years. Everyone added something to the collection.

By the third month, their collection had become huge.

"Look at all this stuff!" Ronnie exclaimed. "There's more here than we can use. Where should we go from here? (Solve-The-Problem and Tell-Me-What's-On-Your-Mind Questions) We can't see and do *everything* in these brochures."

"That's for sure," Carol added. "We'll have to decide what we will do. (Support-Their-Thinking Statement — giving additional information) Any suggestions?" (Solve-The-Problem and Tell-Me-What's-On-Your-Mind Questions)

Michelle was the first to reply: "We could each trace the route and see which of the places we want to visit are near it. Then we can make a list of what we want to see."

"Yeah," Stephen continued, "and we can each put them in order of how important they are to us."

"I know you'd like to see all the places you've found out about," said Carol (Walk-In-Their-Shoes Statement). "We only have two months, so we can't see everything in the United States. (Support-Their-Thinking Statement — giving additional information) You can choose five places each. List them in order of how important they are to you in case we can't see all those on your lists." (Do-It-This-Way Statement)

"That's a good idea," Stephen said.

Deborah Beth added, "I've already got my places picked out!"

"How can we mark them on the map so we all know who wants to see what?" asked Carol. (Tell-Me-What's-On-Your-Mind Question)

"Let's use the colored pins. Each of us can have a different color," Deborah Beth suggested.

"I want blue," Stephen said. "That's the Toronto Blue Jays' color."

"That's a good idea," Ronnie agreed. (Support-Their-Thinking Statement — total agreement) "Now what colors do the rest of you want?" (Give-Me-Specific-Information Question)

The family meeting ended with each child picking a color. Later that evening, the children put their pins in the proper places on the map. Over the next few days the family filled in more details. Carol and Ronnie went over all of them with the children.

To the four children, it seemed like the time to start the trip would never come. To Ronnie and Carol, who had much to do to get prepared, the time went far too quickly.

As the day to begin packing approached, the parents called another family meeting:

"We've all got our sights to see and we've all saved our spending money. Now what will we pack? (Solve-The-Problem Question) We can each take two bags. We can also take a bag with things to do in the van while we're traveling. (Walk-In-Their-Shoes and Look-On-The-Bright-Side Statements) Any ideas?" Carol asked. (Tell-Me-What's-On-Your-Mind Question)

The children thought quietly for a few minutes.

"I want to take one of my favorite travel games," Deborah Beth said.

"That's a good idea," Ronnie agreed. (Catch-Them-Doing-It-Right Statement) "What do you think, Stephen?" (Tell-Me-What's-On-Your-Mind Question)

"I'm going to take my boombox!"

"I know how much you like your music," Ronnie said. (Walk-In-Their-Shoes Statement) "It's too noisy for the van. (Support-Their-Thinking Statement — additional information) Remember, there are five other people in there too. You can take your Walkman® if you want — it has earphones." (Do-It-This-Way Statement)

"We can all take our Walkmans® with us," Andrew said approvingly.

Over the next couple of days, the children packed their gear. The day before the big adventure, Carol and the two younger children checked off the list as Ronnie, Andrew, and Michelle loaded the van.

The children had converted their spending money into traveler's checks earlier in the week, and except for a few dollars they carried themselves, the money was placed with the "Bank of Mom" until needed. Carol and Ronnie (using lots of Solve-The-Problem Questions) had worked with the children to help them plan what they would spend. They would have enough for the special things they wanted to do and for any souvenirs they might want to buy.

> "Now then," Ronnie said, "before we get to bed, we need to make one more decision. Because we're going to leave early in the morning, let's decide now who's going to sit where. Mom and I will sit up front." (Solve-The-Problem Question)

> "I want to sit up with Michelle," said Deborah Beth. "All the boys want to talk about is baseball."

> "What do you think, Michelle? Is that all right with you if you girls sit together?" Carol asked. (Give-Me-Specific-Information Question)

> "Sure. I don't care, just as long as I don't have to sit in the back."

> "Thanks, Michelle," Carol said.

> "We're off to a good start," Ronnie added approvingly. (Catch-Them-Doing-It-Right) "What about you boys?" (Tell-Me-What's-On-Your-Mind Question)

> Surprisingly, both boys agreed.

"Super! We'll have a great time if we keep working together like this," said Ronnie. "Thanks, everyone. (Catch-Them-Doing-It-Right Statement) Now let's get to bed!"

The trip was better than anyone had hoped for. Today, over the couch in the family room, hangs the map of that trip, complete with a label for each place the family visited. Each child's journal describes the many unforgettable experiences they had. No visitor enters their home without seeing the giant map on the family room wall. As each new guest asks about it, one of the family is only too happy to share the adventure. The entire family will talk about this trip for many years to come. You can be sure that even the children's children and grandchildren will hear about it.

Not every family has such a grand adventure. Nevertheless, every family can have an unforgettable adventure of their own. They have to go no farther than a local park, a nearby river or lake, a museum, or even their own home. A picnic on the floor during a rainy day can be a lot of fun, as can putting blankets over a few chairs and "camping out" indoors with children.

One time my dad hung fruit of all kinds on a "magic tree" in the backyard just after my brother left for school one day. Imagine, as a small child, coming home and seeing the tree full of apples, oranges, pears, peaches, and a banana. To him, that *was* magic! Dad really knew how to make being a kid fun. To this day, I have great memories of the delight my brother and I took in the wading pool my dad made from an old mortar box. As a plasterer, he had used the box for hand-mixing materials on job sites. No fancier pool could have been more fun for us!

Learning to be a child again is half the journey. Using the *12 Communication Skills for Effective Parenting* makes it easier. Plan an adventure for your children. They will remember it for a lifetime! Even now, I can smell the cookies Mother helped us make on weekends, and the clip-clop of his horse still echoes in my ears as I remember Norm's bread wagon that Mom and Dad let me ride to school each noon hour. Great memories are born in small moments. Enjoy them with your children.

SUMMING UP AND LOOKING BACK

Whether you are a permissive, authoritarian, or authoritative parent is up to you.

Authoritative (Our Way) parenting *may* be the most supportive. Some parents decided long ago that they prefer sharing decisions with their children and disagree with parents who don't. My Way and Your Way parents also raise responsibly independent children. After all, western society thrives on diversity.

Whatever their preferred style, parents who *say what they mean and mean what they say* usually raise secure and confident children. When they feel secure, children feel free to explore and to learn from their environment. The congruency and consistency of your parenting are important sources of your child's sense of security. That is why this book encourages you to begin *Being the Parent YOU Want to Be*.

APPENDIXES

A. The 12 Communication Skills for Effective Parenting

B. Feeling Words

C. Sample Worksheet 1: My Perceived Parenting Style

D. Sample Worksheet 2: Who Decides?

E. Sample Worksheet 3: Factors in Decision Making

F. Sample Worksheet 4A: Summary Table for Worksheets 2 and 3

G. Sample Worksheet 4B: My Actual Parenting Style

H. Sample Worksheet 5: Are You Congruent?

I. Sample Worksheet 6: Congruency Checkup

APPENDIX A

The 12 Communication Skills for Effective Parenting

SKILLS FOR DISCOVERING WHAT'S ON YOUR CHILD'S MIND

1. Tell-Me-What's-On-Your-Mind Question (TWM)
2. Give-Me-Specific-Information Question (GSI)
3. What-You-Meant Statement (WYM)
4. Think-It-Over Statement (TIO)

SKILLS FOR OVERCOMING YOUR CHILD'S OBJECTIONS

5. Look-On-The-Bright-Side Statement (LOBS)
6. Walk-In-Their-Shoes Statement (WITS)
7. Support-Their-Thinking Statement (STT)
8. Catch-Them-Doing-It-Right Statement (CTDR)

SKILLS FOR SOLVING PROBLEMS AND MAKING DECISIONS WITH YOUR CHILD

9. Solve-The-Problem Question (STP)
10. This-Is-The-Deal Statement (TTD)
11. Out-Of-Bounds Statement (OB)
12. Do-It-This-Way Statement (DITW)

APPENDIX B
Feeling Words

Positive Words

able	impregnable
active	independent
adequate	indestructible
alive	intense
ambitious	jolly
amused	joyful
enthusiastic	joyous
assertive	jubilant
aware	lighthearted
blissful	loved
bold	loving
brave	lucky
bubbly	marvelous
calm	memorable
capable	merry
cheerful	mighty
compassionate	motherly
confident	overjoyed
consistent	peaceful
content	pleasant
courageous	pleased
delighted	positive
determined	powerful
ecstatic	productive
elated	proud
enduring	reliable
energetic	relieved
enthralled	satisfied
everlasting	spirited
excited	secure
exuberant	strong
fine	super
firm	surprised
forceful	thankful
formidable	thrilled
fortunate	tickled
fulfilled	tranquil
gentle	up
glad	uplifted
gleeful	vibrant
glorious	wonderful
good	
great	
happy	
healthy	

Negative Words

afraid	downtrodden	mournful
agitated	exasperated	negative
aggravated	exhausted	out of it
alarmed	fearful	outraged
angry	fed up	painful
anguished	flustered	panicky
annoyed	forgetful	perplexed
anxious	fragile	petrified
apathetic	frantic	powerless
appalled	frightened	provoked
apprehensive	frustrated	rattled
bad	furious	remorseful
baffled	gloomy	revengeful
befuddled	glum	run down
bewildered	grieved	sad
bored	hateful	silly
bothered	helpless	shaky
burdened	hopeless	shy
burned-up	horrified	sore
confounded	hostile	sorry
confused	hurt	spiteful
cross	ill	stunned
crushed	inadequate	terrible
deflated	incapable	terrified
dejected	ineffective	trapped
despairing	infuriated	troubled
despondent	intimidated	turned off
disappointed	irate	uneasy
disconcerted	irked	unfit
disenchanted	irritated	unloved
disgruntled	jumpy	unsure
disoriented	left out	unwanted
displeased	leery	upset
disgusted	lonely	useless
dismayed	lost	weak
distracted	low	worn out
distraught	mad	worried
distressed	mean	
distrustful	melancholy	
disturbed	miffed	
doubtful	miserable	
down	mistrustful	
downcast	mixed up	
downhearted	moody	

APPENDIX C

Sample Worksheet 1: My Perceived Parenting Style

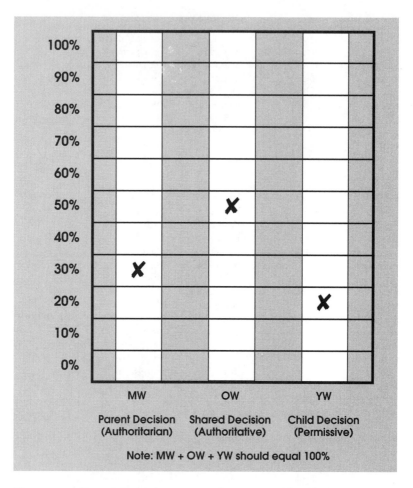

These samples are actual responses from one of the author's workshop participants. This participant had two preschoolers.

APPENDIX D

Sample Worksheet 2: Who Decides?

Next to each statement below, show the percentage of time you:
1) Keep decision-making authority.
2) Share decision-making authority with your children.
3) Give decision-making authority to your children.

When added together, the three columns across each row should total 100%.

Example:
Who decides how to budget
the family income?   85%   10%   5%

	MW Parent Decision	OW Shared Decision	YW Child Decision
1. Who decides what you will eat at mealtimes?	85%	10%	5%
2. Who chooses when and where your family will go for vacation?	60%	30%	10%
3. Who sets the rules for the way your children act at home?	50%	40%	10%
4. Who decides what happens when the kids break these rules?	90%	10%	0%
5. Who decides who will do which chores?	60%	30%	10%
6. Who picks your children's friends?	10%	10%	80%
7. Who decides what your family will do on your vacations?	20%	60%	20%
8. Who chooses your children's clothes and hairstyles?	10%	10%	80%
9. Who decides by what time your kids have to be home in the evening?	10%	80%	10%
10. Who sets bedtimes?	60%	30%	10%
Totals:	455	310	235

APPENDIX E

Sample Worksheet 3: Factors in Decision Making

Next to each statement below, show the percentage of time you:
    1) Keep decision-making authority.
    2) Share decision-making authority with your children.
    3) Give decision-making authority to your children.

When added together, the three columns across each row should total 100%.

Example:
The making of rules in our home is usually a: 70%   20%   10%

	MW Parent Decision	OW Shared Decision	YW Child Decision
1. My children would like more:	0%	10%	90%
2. Because of the age and maturity of my children, I tend more toward:	10%	50%	40%
3. Because of the problems I deal with, I favor:	10%	50%	40%
4. Because I am concerned about my children, I prefer:	50%	30%	20%
5. Because I work, or I am short of time, I prefer:	50%	30%	20%
6. Pressure from others, such as my husband/wife, influences me toward:	50%	30%	20%
7. The way friends treat their children makes me favor:	40%	30%	30%
8. How my parents raised me makes me want to use:	60%	30%	10%
9. If I didn't have to consider anything else, I would choose:	20%	60%	20%
10. Day-to-day I lean toward:	50%	30%	20%
Totals:	340	350	310

APPENDIX F
Sample Worksheet 4A:
Summary Table for Worksheets 2 and 3

	MW Parent Decision (Authoritarian)	OW Shared Decision (Authoritative)	YW Child Decision (Permissive)	Work- sheet Totals
Worksheet 2	455	310	235	1,000
Worksheet 3	340	350	310	1,000
Totals for Worksheets 2 and 3	795	660	545	2,000
Divided by 2	397.50	330	272.50	1,000
Divided by 10 (round off to nearest whole number and show as a percentage)	40%	33%	27%	100%

APPENDIX G

Sample Worksheet 4B: My Actual Parenting Style

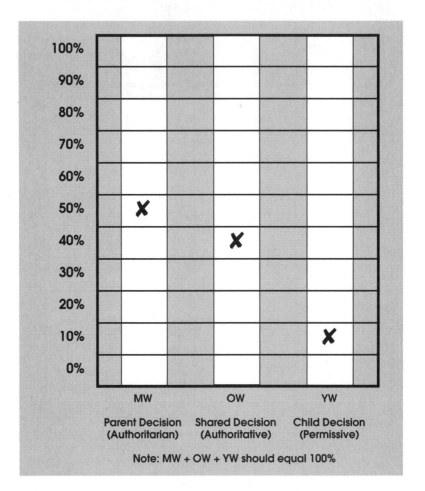

Note: MW + OW + YW should equal 100%

APPENDIX H

Sample Worksheet 5: Are You Congruent?

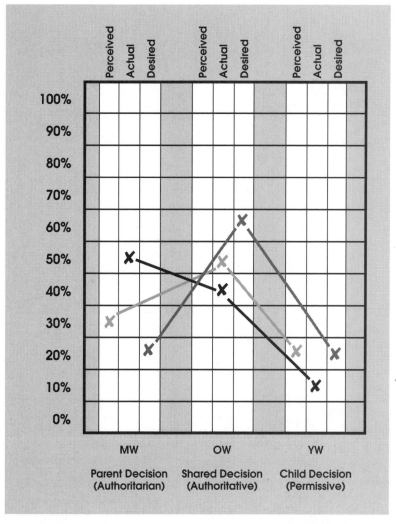

Key: ▬ Perceived Parenting Style   ▬ Actual Parenting Style
     ▬ Desired Parenting Style

APPENDIX I

Sample Worksheet 6: Congruency Checkup (100 observations made)

	No. of Observations	MW	Percentages OW	YW
Skills for Discovering What's On Your Child's Mind				
Tell-Me-What's-On-Your-Mind Question	⊬⊬ /		6%	
Give-Me-Specific-Information Question	⊬⊬ ////	9%		
What-You-Meant Statement	⊬⊬			5%
Think-It-Over Statement	/		1%	
Skills for Overcoming Your Child's Objections				
Look-On-The-Bright-Side Statement	⊬⊬ ////			9%
Walk-In-Their-Shoes Statement				
Pointed to success	////		4%	
Another direction			0%	
Support-Their-Thinking Statement				
Total support	/		1%	
Gave additional information	⊬⊬ //			7%
Catch-Them-Doing-It-Right Statement	⊬⊬ //		7%	
Skills for Solving Problems and Making Decisions With Your Child				
Solve-The-Problem Question				
Asked for solutions:				
broad solutions	/		1%	
narrow solutions	⊬⊬ //	7%		
very narrow solutions			0%	
Offered choices:				
equal choices	⊬⊬ //		7%	
limited choices	⊬⊬		5%	
Hobson's Choice	⊬⊬ /	6%		
This-Is-The-Deal Statement				
Parent acts first	/		1%	
Child acts first	⊬⊬ //	7%		
Out-Of-Bounds Statement	⊬⊬ ///	8%		
Do-It-this-Way Statement	⊬⊬ ////	9%		
Totals: MW + OW + YW = 100%	100	46%	33%	21%

BIBLIOGRAPHY

Page, G.S. (1986). Effectiveness of skills of *Project TEACH*™ as reported by parents. Unpublished research paper.

Page, G.S. (1972, June). Suggestions for an alternative philosophy of education. *The Educational Courier*. This article discusses at length the concept of "responsible independence."

Page, G.S. (1993). *Winning in everyday relationships*. Unpublished manuscript.

Smith, J.M. & Smith, D.E.P. (1976). *Child management: A program for parents and teachers*. Champaign, IL: Research Press.

INDEX

Note: Page numbers in italics indicate worksheet or table displays.

ABOUT THE AUTHOR

Gary Screaton Page, M.Ed. is an award-winning author, speaker, seminar leader, entrepreneur, and ordained minister. He is the husband of Rotraud, the father of Jason and Deidre, father-in-law to their spouses Tamara and Trevor respectively, and grandfather of Austin and Kirstyn. For more than 36 years, Gary Page has taught students from primary grades through college, working with thousands of children and their parents. Gary was also an educational consultant for children's television and has appeared on many national television and radio programs.

For several years, Gary Page was a professional development instructor for Performance Learning Systems, teaching graduate teacher education courses *PRIDE*™ and *Project TEACH*™ (upon which the 12 skills covered in *Being the Parent YOU Want to Be* are based). With Carol Weir, Gary Page is the coauthor of *Being the Parent YOU Want to Be Facilitator Guide* that provides a workshop for teaching the skills in *Being the Parent YOU Want to Be* to parents and teachers.

To have Gary Screaton Page speak at your next meeting, workshop, seminar or conference, call the PLS Presenters Group at 800-757-3878 or 706-342-7952.

Being the Parent YOU Want to Be:
12 Communication Skills for Effective Parenting
by Gary Screaton Page, M.Ed.

Full-color cover
346 pages
Illustrations

Positive communication is the key to friendly, trusting, and caring relationships between parents and children. These practical and useful skills improve relations with your children and bring harmony to your home.

Gary Page's *Being the Parent YOU Want to Be* lets you select the parenting style that works best for you: Authoritative, Permissive, or anything in between. With the skills in this book, you become a more effective parent using your own parenting styles and values.

The 12 Communication Skills of Effective Parenting are presented in an accessible, straightforward manner, with plenty of examples, sample conversations, and practice. Using these skills, you encourage your children to speak openly, make good decisions, improve self-esteem, increase responsibility, and develop a deeper understanding of the consequences of their behavior.

Order directly from Performance Learning Systems through the PLS Bookstore. Quantity discounts available.
> PLS Bookstore
> 224 Church Street
> Nevada City, CA 95959
> Retail orders:
>> 800-506-9996
>> Fax: 530-265-8629
>> Full-Order Web Site: www.plsbookstore.com
>> E-mail: info@plsbookstore.com
> Bookstores, libraries, distributors, other wholesalers:
>> 800-255-8412
>> Fax: 530-265-8629
>> E-mail: bbpls@gv.net

Being the Parent YOU Want to Be Facilitator Guide

by Gary Screaton Page, M.Ed. and Carol Ann Weir

84 pages
48 reproducible pages

Being the Parent YOU Want to Be Facilitator Guide presents a four-session workshop that will help parents improve their parent-child relationships. Working with his guide, you can prepare a highly effective workshop that will enable parents to identify their parenting styles, learn the 12 communication skills, and leave each session with something new to try at home. These workshops could be provided for parents, teachers, day-care providers, and all others who work with children.

The Facilitator Guide includes:
Four easy to facilitate workshop sessions.
Hour-by-hour, step-by-step directions.
Points to cover in each workshop.
Role-plays for practicing the communication skills.
48 pages of reproducible materials.
Ideas for workshop setup, materials, time schedules,
    and equipment.
Reading assignments, an introductory letter for workshop participants,
    and an evaluation form.

In the words of one parent who attended the workshop sessions:
"Thanks for both the book and the course. I have not yet mastered all of the techniques, but I am on my way. Communication with my son has significantly improved, and I now have tools to deal with the rest of his growing up years!"

Order directly from Performance Learning Systems through the PLS Bookstore.
    PLS Bookstore
    224 Church Street
    Nevada City, CA 95959
    Retail orders:
        800-506-9996
        Fax: 530-265-8629
        Full-Order Web Site: www.plsbookstore.com
        E-mail: info@plsbookstore.com
    Bookstores, libraries, distributors, other wholesalers:
        Contact Independent Publishers Group (IPG), Ingram, or
        Baker and Taylor. ISBN 1-892334-08-9

Discover Your Children's Learning Styles!
Using The Kaleidoscope Profile™

Student profiles (grades 3 - 12)
Adult profiles
   (Standard and Educator)
Directions and Applications booklet

The Student version of the **Kaleidoscope Profile**™ is a useful tool that will give you information about how your children learn and what they value. The Standard version will tell how you learn and work best so you can compare your styles with those of your children.

The profile uses colorful stickers to indicate 12 different learning and working styles. The sticker approach to profiling is a vast improvement over paper-and-pencil profiles. Everyone finds this profile fun to take and easy to score.

When you know how your children learn best, you can help them:
- improve the way they study.
- learn better.
- prepare for tests.
- figure out how to listen in class and take notes.
- relate better to teachers, siblings, and friends.
- convey their learning styles to teachers and tutors.
- And more!

As one parent said: "Understanding my son's learning styles – and my own – gave me useful tools for working with him at home. Now he can use learning techniques that match his style."

Order directly from Performance Learning Systems through the PLS Bookstore. Four versions of the profile are available:
- Student (grades 3-6)   • Standard (adult and college students)
- Student (grades 7-12) • Educator (for classroom teachers)
   800-506-9996
   Fax: 530-265-8629
   Full-Order Web Site: www.plsbookstore.com
   E-mail: info@plsbookstore.com